Personal Injury Litigation

Available titles in this series include:

Agricultural Tenancies
Angela Sydenham

Change of Name
Nasreen Pearce

Child Care and Protection
Barbara Mitchels with Helen James

Debt Recovery in the Courts
John Kruse

Partnership and LLP Law
Elspeth Berry

Procedure in Civil Courts and Tribunals
John Bowers QC and Eleena Misra

Residential Tenancies
Richard Colbey and Niamh O'Brien

Termination of Employment
John Bowers QC and Carol Davis

 Wildy Practice Guides

Personal Injury Litigation

Fourth edition

Gordon Exall

Wildy, Simmonds and Hill Publishing

Contains public sector information licensed under the Open Government Licence v1.0

The right of Gordon Exall to be identified as the author of this Work has been asserted by him in accordance with sections 77 and 78 of the Copyright, Designs and Patents Act 1988

First published in Great Britain 2011 by Wildy, Simmonds & Hill Publishing

Website: www.wildy.com

Exall, Gordon

Personal Injury Litigation, 4th edition (Wildy Practice Guides series)

British Library Cataloguing in Publication Data

A catalogue record for this book is available from the British Library

ISBN 978-0854900-862

Typeset in Baskerville MT Pro and Optima LT by Cornubia Press Ltd

Printed and bound by CPI Group (UK) Ltd, Croydon, CR0 4YY

Contents

Appendices

List of Forms and Precedents

Preface

The first edition of this book was written in 1988 by Nick Saunders, who had taught me civil procedure when I was a student. I wrote the second edition in 1992 and the third in 2002 when massive changes were made by the introduction of the Civil Procedure Rules. The changes to personal injury practice continue. The book now includes specific chapters on limitation, fatal accidents, the road traffic accident process and drafting witness statements. There is now a section on provisional damages, Part 36 offers have replaced 'payments into court' and I have included a short chapter on avoiding the pitfalls. I aim to keep this book a simple guide to the key elements of personal injury litigation – an area which is becoming more complex, particularly with the introduction of the computer-led road traffic procedure.

Traditionally, the forms and precedents were separate and at the back of the book. The fact has to be faced that the forms are now an integral part of the litigation process. Consequently, they are now in the body of the text integral to the relevant chapter, where the reader is able to refer to them directly. In particular, the forms are essential to an understanding of the Road Traffic Accident Protocol. In order to understand the requirements of Form RTA 1 it is necessary to see it (see para 6.11.1). The reader is not left without guidance; for instance, the checklist of information required to complete RTA 1 is at para 6.6.2.

I have to thank my research assistant Charlotte Nevison for her assistance, particularly at the proofreading stage. My family always look for a mention of their names (and I suspect have never read beyond that point), so I thank my wife Rosemary and my children Jonathan, Thomas, Elizabeth and Ben for their encouragement and distraction.

The law is stated as at 16 June 2011.

1 Basic Information: Liability

The starting point for most personal injury actions is the law of negligence. However, liability can be affected by statutory duties. Practitioners must be particularly aware of the statutory provisions relating to employer's liability, including the fact that strict liability or a reversal of the burden of proof can attach in a large number of circumstances. Statutory duties also apply in relation to accidents on the highway, cases involving defective products and actions relating to animals.

1.1   General principles

1.1.1   Negligence

Most personal injury actions are pleaded in negligence. Accordingly, the claimant must show the existence of a duty of care owed by the defendant to, and breach of, that duty causing the claimant to suffer damage which was not too legally remote.

The duty is a duty to take reasonable care. The flexibility of the standard is shown by situations such as sporting events, where it may be easier for the defendant to show that he or she took reasonable care to avoid harm to players (*Condon v Basi* [1985] 2 All ER 457) and, in the case of children, the standard is adjusted for the child's age (*Gorely v Codd* [1967] 1 WLR 19). Proof of breach of the standard may be helped by the maxim *res ipsa loquitur* if the accident was caused by something under the defendant's control (such as a car) and was something that would not normally happen without negligence (such as the car running into a tree). The court may give the claimant judgment in the absence of contrary evidence (*Bergin v David Wickes Television Ltd* [1994] PIQR P167). However, the onus of proof remains on the claimant (*Ng Chun Pui v Lee Chuen Tat* [1988] RTR 298).

The basic test of causation is whether the claimant's harm would not have occurred but for the defendant's negligence. However, several causes may satisfy this test. Where they each contribute to the harm themselves, the claimant can sue all those who caused the injury.

Alternatively, the claimant can sue any one of them, leaving that defendant to recover from the other persons at fault a contribution or indemnity for the damages he or she has paid to the claimant (Civil Liability (Contribution) Act 1978). In any event, the issue of who to sue and whether they are, in fact, responsible for the injury, is one that must be considered carefully prior to issue. Normally, these issues would be clarified by discussions and negotiations that take place under the Pre-Action Protocol.

1.1.2   Breach of statutory duty

Some statutes give a claimant a right to sue for damages if the duties set out in the statute (or associated statutory instruments) are breached. For the claimant to be able to recover compensation for breach of statutory duty it must be shown that the statute is intended to create a right to compensation, that the claimant is within the type of persons whom the statute intended to benefit and that the damage was of the type that the statute was intended to guard against. These questions can only be decided in the context of the particular statute.

However, the central point that practitioners need to be aware of is that a claim for breach of statutory duty need not necessarily involve 'fault' or 'blame' as is required in negligence. The central issue is whether the duty has been breached. If the statute has been breached, then liability can be established, even if the injury was not foreseeable or the defendant is not to blame in any way. So in *Stark v The Post Office* [2000] All ER (D) 276, the post office was liable when the brakes on one of its bicycles failed because the duty to 'maintain' work equipment, imposed by the Provision and Use of Work Equipment Regulations 1992 (SI 1992/ 2932), was an absolute duty. If the equipment failed, there was a breach of duty despite the fact that the defendant had done everything it could reasonably do to maintain the cycle. This duty applied even if the failure was of a minor part of the machinery.

Causation must also be established as in negligence cases and the defence of contributory negligence is available. However, the courts are enjoined to be aware that the very reason these Regulations exist is because people are careless and that the Regulations impose a duty that is higher than the law of negligence.

1.1.3   Vicarious liability

In certain circumstances the law can hold someone liable for the negligence or breach of duty of another. The most common circumstance is where the negligent person is employed and the injury is caused whilst he or she is working in the course of his or her employment. To hold the employer liable, the person committing the tort must have been employed under a contract *of* service, not a contract *for* services, and acting in the course of the employment, that is, on the employer's business and not a 'frolic of his own'.

Where there is vicarious liability, the employer and employee are jointly and severally liable to the claimant. Since the employer under the Employers' Liability (Compulsory Insurance) Act 1969 must be insured against third party claims, it is common to sue only the employer, having first obtained an agreement from the employer's insurers or its solicitors that vicarious liability will not be disputed.

In *Lister v Hesley Hall Ltd* [2001] UKHL 22, the House of Lords held that a local authority was vicariously liable for acts of sexual abuse carried out by the warden of a school boarding house. The test was held to be whether the perpetrator's torts were so closely connected with his employment that it would be fair and just to hold the defendant vicariously liable.

1.1.4   Liability for acts of independent contractors

It is normally enough if the defendant has employed apparently competent contractors (*Cassidy v Minister of Health* [1951] 2 KB 343) unless the defendant was under a non-delegable duty to ensure that care was taken, such as an employer or, in certain circumstances, a highway authority. However, when the occupier wishes for something dangerous to be done on the land, there is a duty to take reasonable care in selecting 'competent' contractors (*Bottomley v Todmorden Cricket Club* [2003] EWCA Civ 1575).

1.2   Road accidents

1.2.1   Substantive law

A user of the road has a duty to take reasonable care to avoid injury to other road users. The usual arguments are over whether the driver's duty of care to other road users has been broken, whether any breach has caused the claimant's loss and as to any contributory negligence by the claimant.

Where the defendant has been convicted of a relevant driving offence, the burden of proof is effectively reversed by section 11 of the Civil Evidence Act 1968. This requires the defendant to show that the conviction was wrong or irrelevant, for example, because the offence of driving with defective brakes was one of strict liability and the defendant had no warning of the brake failure.

The standard expected is that of the reasonably careful and competent qualified driver (*Nettleship v Weston* [1971] 2 QB 691). The driver must anticipate the negligence of others where experience suggests that this is common, but can assume that generally other motorists will obey the fundamental rules of the road, such as stopping at red traffic lights (*Tremayne v Hill* [1987] RTR 131, CA). Pedestrians also have a duty to take reasonable care (*Fitzgerald v Lane* [1988] 2 All ER 961, HL). *The Highway Code* is admissible to show the practice of reasonably careful road users (section 30 of the Road Traffic Act (RTA) 1988).

Where several vehicles are involved, it may be very difficult to establish exactly which vehicles did what damage. In order to avoid this type of problem, the court may look at the matter broadly as being one event (*Fitzgerald v Lane* [1988] 2 All ER 961, HL).

1.2.2   Insurance and compensation schemes

Drivers using a motor vehicle on a public road should have insurance against claims by third parties for personal injuries and death(s). Judgments for such losses can be enforced against the insurers, even if the insurers were entitled to or have, in fact, avoided the policy, for example, for misrepresentation by their insured. Notice must have been given before or within 7 days of taking proceedings (section 151 of the RTA 1988). Enforcement against insurers is also possible if the third party has gone bankrupt or into liquidation (Third Parties (Rights against Insurers) Act 1930).

However, this will not apply if the driver was uninsured, for example, because the policy was allowed to lapse or if, at the time of the accident, the use of the vehicle was not covered by the policy. In this situation, the judgment will have to be enforced against the Motor Insurers' Bureau (MIB) under the uninsured driver agreement. Appropriate notification must be given to the MIB and a very strict regime of notification is in place.

If the driver cannot be traced but it is possible to show that the accident was the fault of the untraced driver, a claim can be made to the MIB under the untraced driver agreement. The MIB will instruct a member insurer to investigate the claim – liability and quantum having to be proved in the usual way. There is an appeal by way of arbitration to a QC.

If the accident was the result of a deliberate attempt to injure, the uninsured driver agreement will apply but not the untraced driver agreement. An application to the Criminal Injuries Compensation Authority (CICA) can, however, be made.

Under the insurance policy, the insurers will normally have rights to be informed of any claims against the insured person and to nominate solicitors to deal with those claims. If they pay a claim under the policy, for example, for repairs to their insured's vehicle, they have the right of subrogation, that is, to take proceedings in their insured's name against any other person who may be liable to recover the amount paid.

1.3   Dangerous premises

The liability of occupiers to lawful visitors is regulated by the Occupiers' Liability Act 1957. The 'common duty of care' owed to all visitors (section 2(1)) is very similar to the common law of negligence. The degree of care will vary with the type of visitor, so occupiers must expect children to be less careful than adults (section 2(3)(a)). The occupier is entitled to expect that a person in the exercise of his or her calling will guard against any special risks ordinarily incidental to it (but see *Ogwo v Taylor* [1987] 3 WLR 1145, HL).

Finally, where the damage *results* from the negligence of an independent contractor, the occupier will generally not be liable if reasonable care was taken in selecting and supervising the contractor (*Ferguson v Welsh* [1987] 3 All ER 777, HL) but may be liable if reasonable care was not taken and a dangerous activity was planned (*Bottomley v Todmorden Cricket Club* [2003] EWCA Civ 1575).

The liability of occupiers to persons other than lawful visitors, for example, trespassers, is governed by the Occupiers' Liability Act 1984. This imposes a lower standard of care to those who are not lawful visitors to the premises (a 'non-visitor'). The occupier will owe a duty to take reasonable care to see that the non-visitor does not suffer injury only if: (1) the occupier ought to have known of the danger; (2) the non-visitor was likely to be in the vicinity; and (3) it is reasonable to expect the non-visitor to be offered some protection. The courts have been reluctant to impose a duty in circumstances where the danger was obvious and the injured person accepted that danger (*Darby v The National Trust* [2001] EWCA Civ 189 and *Tomlinson v Congleton Borough Council* [2003] UKHL 47).

1.3.1   Duty to maintain a highway

The highway authority is under a statutory duty to maintain a highway (section 41 of the Highways Act 1980). The highway authority is usually the local county council or the metropolitan district council. A duty is owed to all persons who it is reasonably foreseeable might be affected.

Where a contractor is engaged to perform work on a highway, the highway authority cannot delegate its legal responsibility. The statutory duty found in section 41 is in general non-delegable (*Hardaker v Idle District Coucil* [1986] 1 QB 335).

To render a highway authority liable, it must be proven that there was a reasonably foreseeable danger. Minor irregularities are unlikely to create liability. Generally, the rule is that there has to be at least a one-inch difference in the level of a pavement. Where there is a defect on a carriageway, then the defect usually has to be much larger (*McLoughlin v Strathclyde Regional Council* [1992] SLT 959). A highway authority also has the duty to ensure that safe passage along the highway is not endangered by snow or ice.

Once it has been proven that there was a reasonably foreseeable danger, then the burden shifts to the highway authority to prove that it is not liable. It must show that it did all that was reasonably required to ensure that the highway was safe. The court will take into account what type of highway it is, what maintenance would be expected for that highway, whether the local authority knew of the defect, the authority's policy for inspecting defects and any warnings.

1.4   Dangerous products

Where a dangerous product causes injury, a claimant has a number of potential claims: in negligence, in breach of contract or under the Consumer Protection Act 1987. A purchaser of a defective product that causes injury may have a remedy in contract against the seller. The Sale of Goods Act 1979 imposes into sales, in the course of a business, terms of reasonable quality and reasonable fitness for purpose.

The Consumer Protection Act (CPA) 1987 gives a cause of action to anyone injured by a defective product. Although the claimant may not have had any contract with the defendant, and may be unable to prove that the defendant was at fault, the producer (that is, the manufacturer of the whole or the relevant component of the product), any 'own-branders' who put their name on the product, or the first importers into the European Union can be held liable. If none of these is identifiable, the claimant can sue the supplier (section 2).

A product is defective if its safety is not such as persons generally are entitled to expect, having regard to any warnings given with the product (section 3(1)). Damage includes death, personal injury and loss of or damage to property, excluding the defective product itself, exceeding £275 (section 5(1)).

1.5   Accidents at work

Employers may be liable vicariously for the negligence of employees acting in the course of their employment, personally for breach of non-delegable common law duties, or for breach of statutory duty. Vicarious liability is dealt with at para 1.1.3. Finally, apart from holding the employer liable, it may be possible to seek a payment from the state under the Pneumoconiosis etc (Workers' Compensation) Act 1979 in the case of certain prescribed diseases.

1.5.1   Common law duties

The employer owes personal, non-delegable duties to employees (*McDermid v Nash Dredging and Reclamation* [1987] AC 906, HL) to provide safe plant and machinery (section 1(1) of the Employers' Liability (Defective Equipment) Act 1969), to provide a safe place of work, to provide a safe system of work and to provide reasonably competent and properly instructed staff. These duties, however, are only to do what is reasonable and employees, too, are expected to take reasonable care of their own safety (*Smith v Scott Bowyers* [1986] IRLR 315, CA).

1.5.2   Statutory duties

As a result of EEC Directives, many accidents at the workplace come within the ambit of one of the following regulations. The most commonly used provisions are the Management of Health and Safety at Work Regulations 1999 (SI 1999/3242), the Workplace (Health, Safety and Welfare) Regulations 1992 (W(HS&W)) (SI 1992/3004), the Provision and Use of Work Equipment Regulations 1998 (PUWE) (SI 1998/2306), the Personal Protective Equipment at Work Regulations 1992 (PPER) (SI 1992/2966) and the Manual Handling Operations Regulations 1992 (MHOR) (SI 1992/2793). More specific duties are imposed by the Work at Height Regulations 2005 (SI 2005/735) and the Construction (Design and Management Regulations) 2007 (SI 2007/320).

The duties most often relevant are:

(a)   to ensure that work equipment is maintained in an efficient state, in efficient working order and in good repair (regulation 5 of the PUWE). This is an absolute obligation. Even if the equipment is unsafe with no fault at all on the part of the employer, the defendant has breached its obligations (*Stark v The Post Office* [2000] PIQR 105);

(b)   to give information and instructions on the use of work equipment (regulations 8 and 9 of the PUWE);

(c)   to prevent access to dangerous parts of machinery (regulation 11 of the PUWE);

(d)   to ensure that floors, passages and *stairs* are sound, free from obstruction and not slippery (regulation 12 of the W(HS&W));

(e)   to avoid manual handling operations which involve a risk of injury or, if that cannot be avoided, to reduce the risk to the lowest level reasonably practicable (regulation 4 of the MHOR). This does not just apply to lifting injuries; the MHOR apply to any case involving 'handling' a load;

(f)   to avoid working at height. If that work cannot be avoided, the risk must be reduced following the guidelines set out in the Work at Height Regulations 2005 and *Batt v Fontain Motors* [2010] EWCA Civ 863;

(g)   to provide personal protective equipment (PPER) (*Threlfall v Hull City Council* [2010] EWCA Civ 1147).

Duty to carry out a risk assessment

One important matter that must be considered in any claim by an employer is the employer's duty to carry out a suitable and sufficient risk assessment imposed by regulation 4 of the Management of Health and Safety at Work Regulations 1999. This is a mandatory duty. Having carried out a risk assessment, the employer's duty is to take steps to eliminate or reduce the risk of injury applying the principles of prevention. The issue of what risks the employer should know about in its operations is decided by what the employer would have known if it had carried out an adequate risk assessment (*Allison v London Underground* [2008] EWCA Civ 71 and *Threlfall v Hull City Council* [2010] EWCA Civ 1147).

Occupational illness claims

Occupational illness claims such as deafness, asbestos disease, respiratory diseases, vibration white finger and upper-limb disorder are governed by similar common law principles as accidents at work. Issues such as foreseeability and causation are often at the fore. However, considerable attention has to be paid to specific statutory duties. In deafness cases, the Factories Act 1961 (in cases to which that Act applied), the Noise at Work Regulations 1989 (SI 1989/1790) and the Control of Noise at Work Regulations 2005 (SI 2005/1643) are important. In asbestos cases, the Control of Asbestos at Work Regulations 1987 (SI 1987/2115) may come into play. The Control of Vibration at Work Regulations 2005 (SI 2005/1093) are important to vibration white finger cases. Some occupational illness cases relate to work carried out some decades ago. In these cases, careful consideration is needed of the provisions of the Factories Act 1961, in particular of section 29(1) which imposed a duty to keep the workplace safe.

Travel claims

Where the claimant is injured on a 'package'-type holiday, an action may lie against the company that organised that holiday under the provisions of the Package Travel, Package Holidays and Package Tours Regulations 1992 (SI 1992/3288). The travel agent is responsible to the consumer for any damage caused to him or her because of the failures of other parties to perform the contract. However, the question of the standards to be applied is governed by the standards applicable in the country where the accident occurred and not by UK standards (*Wilson v Best Travel* [1993] 1 All ER 353).

Animals

Where an injury is caused by an animal, a claimant may have a claim in negligence against the person responsible. If the injury is caused by an animal of a 'dangerous species', then there is strict liability for injury under the Animals Act 1971. A dangerous species is an animal which is not commonly domesticated in the UK and which has characteristics such that, unless restrained, is likely to cause severe damage. If the animal is not of a dangerous species, then an action can lie under the Animals Act 1971 if the claimant establishes three things required by section 2(2):

(a)   That the damage is of a kind which the animal, unless restrained, was likely to cause or which was likely to be severe.

(b)   That the likelihood of the damage or of its being severe was due to characteristics of the animal which are not normally found in animals of the same species or are not normally found except at particular times or in particular circumstances.

(c)   These characteristics were known to the keeper of the animal, the keeper's employee or, where the keeper is the head of the household, another keeper of the animal who is a member of the household and under the age of 16.

Clinical negligence

The difficulties here relate to the standard of care, causation and evidence.

Standard of care

A doctor's duty is not to cure the patient but to conform to the standard of a reasonably competent person exercising and professing to have that skill. It appears that the standard will be that appropriate to the function that the defendant performs: a houseman will be judged by the standard applicable to a junior doctor and not to a consultant (*Witcher v Essex AHA* [1987] 3 QB 730, CA).The doctor must keep up to date with medical practice, but will not be liable if he or she has acted in accordance with a practice accepted as proper by a responsible body of doctors skilled in that area, even if some doctors would have acted differently (*Bolam v Friern Hospital Management Committee* [1952] 2 All ER 118).This applies to all aspects of medicine, including diagnosis, treatment and advice (*Gold v Haringey HA* [1987] 3 All ER 649, CA).

1.6   Causation

Negligence will not be actionable if the claimant would have suffered the harm in any event (*Kay v Ayrshire and Arran Health Board* [1987] 2 All ER 417, HL). If the chance of recovery would otherwise have been less than 50%, the defendant's negligence will not be regarded as causing the loss, and no damages can be awarded: the claimant cannot recover a proportion of the damages for the loss of a chance of recovery less than 50% (*Hotson v East Berkshire HA* [1987] 2 All ER 910, HL). If there are several possible causes, the court cannot in the absence of evidence infer that the negligent one was the cause of the loss (*Washer v Essex AHA* [1988] All ER 871, HL).

1.7   Defences

The claimant has the burden of establishing negligence or breach of statutory duty. A defendant can defend a case on the basis that there was no negligence or breach. There are other defences available and, generally, burden of proof in establishing these defences is on the defendant.

1.7.1   Contributory negligence

The courts can apportion liability where harm has been caused partly by the fault of the defendant and partly by that of the claimant (section 1(1) of the Law Reform (Contributory Negligence) Act 1945).

The defendant must raise the point by pleading it in the defence. It must be shown that the claimant failed to take reasonable care and that this contributed either to the accident or to the damage, for example, by failing to wear a seat belt (*Froom v Butcher* [1976] QB 286).

A motorcyclist who fails to fasten the chin strap of his or her helmet can be contributorily negligent (*Capps v Miller* [1989] 2 All ER 333).

The defence is applied in the light of the claimant's age and physical, but not mental, condition. It is less likely to apply in actions for breach of statutory duty which are designed to protect workers from their own carelessness.

The court reduces the claimant's damages to the extent it thinks just and reasonable, having regard to the claimant's share in the responsibility for the damage, assessed in terms of causation (*Fitzgerald v Lane* [1987] 2 All ER 455, CA) or, more commonly, the parties' relative degree of culpability (*Westwood v The Post Office* [1974] AC 1). It is not possible to have 100% contributory negligence (*Pitts v Hunt* [1991] 1 QB 24).

It has been emphasised that there is a difference between 'momentary inattention' and 'the risks that have been consciously accepted by an employee' (*Sherlock v Chester City Council* [2004] EWCA Civ 210). Therefore, a failure to concentrate will provide a finding of contributory negligence. For example, in *Ellis v Bristol City Council* [2007] EWCA Civ 685, a carer slipped on urine in the care home where she worked, despite there being notices of the hazard in the staffroom and in the corridors. Similarly, in *Griffths v Vauxhall Motors Limited* [2003] EWCA Civ 412, despite its monotonous nature, the claimant was found 50% contributorily negligent for failing to sufficiently grip the tool that he used to tighten around 42 to 84 bolts per hour.

1.7.2   *Volenti non fit injuria*

This means a voluntary agreement by the claimant, made with knowledge of the nature and extent of the risk, to absolve the defendant from legal liability for the results of an unreasonable risk of harm.

Because of economic pressures, *volenti* will rarely be available in employers' liability actions (*ICI v Shatwell* [1965] AC 656). Nor, probably, will it apply to accepting lifts from drunken or incompetent drivers (*Dann v Hamilton* [1939] 1 KB 509). Notices in cars that travel is at the passenger's own risk are ineffective (section 148(3) of the RTA 1972). However, the defence may be available to occupiers, at least with regard to non-visitors (*Titchener v British Railways Board* [1983] 3 All ER 770).

The claimant must have had actual knowledge of both the nature and extent of the risk. However, doctors do not have a duty to warn a patient of all the risks of treatment, but only those that a reasonably careful doctor would mention (*Sidaway v Bethlem Royal Hospital Governors* [1985] 1 All ER 643, HL).

The consent needed for the defence to succeed in negligence actions is not to the risk of injury as such, but to the lack of reasonable care that may produce that risk (*Wooldridge v Sumner* [1963] 2 QB 43). Thus, the defence will not often succeed in ordinary negligence cases; however, see *Morris v Murray* (1990) *The Times,* 18 September, CA.

1.7.3   Exclusion clauses

These are now ineffective in relation to liability for death or personal injury to motor vehicle passengers. Further, attempts to exclude from negligence such liability arising in the course of a business are ineffective (section 2(1) of the Unfair Contract Terms Act 1977), although duties stricter than negligence can be excluded. In respect of other losses, exclusion is valid only if reasonable (section 2(2)).

1.7.4   Illegality

In some circumstances, the defendant may be able to rely on the maxim that a person cannot profit from his or her own wrong (*Cummings v Grainger* [1977] 1 All ER 104, and see *Pitts v Hunt* [1989] 3 WLR 795). Even if the illegality is not a defence to the claim for liability, it can be a defence to some aspects of the claim for damages, so a person who is working unlawfully may not be able to recover damages for loss of earnings (*Hewison v Meridian Shipping* [2002] EWCA Civ 1821, [2003] ICR 766).

1.8   Key points

* Negligence is a breach of the duty to take reasonable care. The burden of proving this lies with the claimant.

* An action for breach of statutory duty can be totally different to an action for negligence. Sometimes the defendant's duty is strict. On other occasions, the burden of proof can be reversed.

* A defendant can defend an action on the basis that he or she was not negligent or in breach of duty. Specific defences such as contributory negligence, illegality and *volenti* have to be pleaded. The burden of proving these specific defences lies on the defendant.

2 Limitation

2.1 General

The first thing that a lawyer instructed by a claimant must consider is the issue of limitation. This is also an important point for defendants since the defence of limitation needs to be specifically pleaded.

Failure by the claimant to issue proceedings within the limitation period and to serve them within a further 4 months is the single biggest cause of professional negligence claims in civil litigation. It is essential for a lawyer to make a prominent diary and file note covering the expiry of these periods and to have a procedure for regularly reviewing all files to check that such dates have not been missed. A master index of such dates, on computer if necessary, is a good back-up.

Limitation must be pleaded by the defendant if it is to be relied on. It is not for the claimant to apply to have the matter dealt with before the action can proceed (*Kennet v Brown* [1998] 2 All ER 600, CA). However, limitation is normally taken as a preliminary point before the substantive issues are tried.

2.2 Basic period

In personal injury actions, the basic period is 3 years from either the date of accrual of the cause of action (that is, when the damage occurs) or, if later, the date of the claimant's knowledge that the injury was significant and attributable to the defendant's breach of duty (section 14(1) of the Limitation Act 1980). An injury is significant if it would have been reasonable to take proceedings in respect of it (section 14(2)). Knowledge includes that which the claimant could reasonably be expected to acquire him- or herself, or with the help of expert advice (section 14(3)).

In the case of a child, the limitation period does not run until the child reaches his or her 18th birthday (however, there are exceptions in relation to actions brought under certain statutes, see below).

A protected party is a person suffering from a disability such that he or she cannot administer his or her own affairs. The limitation period does not start to run until he or she ceases to be a protected party.

2.3   Date of knowledge

The date of knowledge can be controversial. In most accident cases it is easily identifiable as the date of the accident. In disease cases, or cases of sexual abuse, the date of knowledge is often more controversial. The court will consider the factors in section 14 of the Limitation Act 1980; that is, the date the claimant first had knowledge:

(a)   that the injury was significant;

(b)   that the injury was due to the acts or omissions of the defendant;

(c)   of the identity of the defendant;

(d)   of the identity of the person, other than the defendant, alleged to have committed the act or made the omission, and the additional facts supporting the bringing of an action against the defendant.

The fact that the claimant did not know that the defendant's acts or omissions were negligent or represented a breach of duty is irrelevant to the issue of date of knowledge.

In *A v Hoare* [2008] UKHL 6, the House of Lords held that the test of what is 'significant' is an objective test and not one that depends on what a reasonable person would have done and not a person with the specific characteristics of the claimant.

2.4   Overriding the time bar

The court has the discretion to allow an action to proceed after the expiry of the basic period if it is equitable to do so, having regard to the degree to which the time bar prejudices the claimant and the degree to which overriding it will prejudice the defendant (section 33(1)). The court must look at all the circumstances including the length of and reasons for delay, the effect on the cogency of the evidence and any steps the claimant has taken to obtain expert advice. The discretion is unfettered. There is no longer any bar on a claimant, who has issued a first set of proceedings which have been struck out or not served, relying on section 33 when issuing a second set of proceedings (*Horton v Sadler* [2006] UKHL 27).

When considering exercising a discretion under section 33, the court cannot take into account the fact that a defendant loses the limitation defence (*Cain v Francis* [2008] EWCA Civ 1451). The fundamental question is whether it is fair and just in all the circumstances for the action to proceed.

In *A v Hoare* [2008] UKHL 6, the House of Lords held that a more liberal approach to section 33 can be taken in cases of sexual abuse where a claimant may have 'blocked out' the assaults.

2.5 Specific actions

2.5.1 Fatal accidents

Under both the Law Reform (Miscellaneous Provisions) Act 1934 and the Fatal Accidents Act 1976, if the deceased died before the expiry of the limitation period, then a 3-year period runs from the date of death or the date of knowledge of the personal representatives or dependants. When this expires, an application can be made under section 33. If the deceased's limitation period had expired, then the personal representatives or dependants must apply under section 33.

However, different limitation periods can apply for different dependants. In the case of a dependant who is under the age of 18, the limitation period for his or her dependency will not start to run until he or she reaches his or her 18th birthday (section 13 of the Limitation Act 1980). The fact that there are dependants whose action is not statute barred can be an important factor when a court hears a section 33 application in relation to the claims of other dependants whose claims are statute barred (*Richardson v Watson* [2006] EWCA Civ 1662).

2.5.2 Consumer Protection Act 1987

The usual rules apply with an absolute 10-year long stop (Schedule 1 to the CPA 1987).

2.5.3 Compensation schemes

Under both MIB schemes, the time limit is 3 years from the event giving rise to the injury. Under the Criminal Injuries Compensation Scheme, there is a 2-year limit. All the schemes will entertain a late application in exceptional circumstances. In the case of a minor, the MIB must entertain a claim made up to 3 years after the applicant's 18th birthday.

2.5.4   Actions concerning aircraft and ships: unusual limitation periods

Ships and vessels

Care must be taken in cases involving ships and vessels as a 2-year limitation period may apply: see the Merchant Shipping Act 1995 and the Maritime Conventions Act 1911. The term 'vessel' includes hovercrafts.

The time limit runs from the date of disembarkation or, in the case of a death, the date on which the deceased should have disembarked.

Aircraft

A strict 2-year limitation period applies for accidents in and around aircraft: see the Carriage by Air Act 1961. This Act enacts the Warsaw Convention on the Carriage of Goods by Air and the Montreal Convention for the Unification of Certain Rules for International Carriage. At the end of the 2-year period the action is completely extinguished. There is no possibility of the court exercising a discretion under section 33 of the Limitation Act 1980. It is important, therefore, that the claim form and particulars of claim make it clear that the claim is brought.

Embarkation and disembarkation

The accident need not necessarily be on the aircraft itself; the 2-year period applies in relation to accidents that occur when a passenger is embarking or disembarking an aircraft. A passenger who was being taken upstairs to a departure gate in order that she could board an aircraft was held to be embarking and therefore subject to a 2-year limitation period (*Phillips v Air New Zealand* [2002] EWHC 800 (Comm), [2002] 2 Lloyd's Rep 408).

The term 'aircraft' also applies to hot air balloons: see *Laroche v Spirit of Adventure (UK) Ltd* [2009] EWCA Civ 12, in which a claimant who brought an action after 2 years had his claim dismissed because the balloon trip was subject the Convention.

In all such cases (including minors and persons under a disability), the cause of action expires if an action is not brought within the 2-year period.

2.5.5 Accidents abroad

Accidents abroad can be governed by the foreign limitation period and not the English: see the Foreign Limitation Periods Act 1984. Practitioners must be aware of the fact that a different limitation period may apply with different rules for calculating the date of commencement of the limitation period. The fact that a solicitor was ignorant of these requirements does not constitute good grounds for the exercise of the court's discretion to disapply the provisions of this Act (*Harley v Smith* [2010] EWCA Civ 78).

2.6 Key points

- The issue of limitation is a point that must be considered at the outset by both claimant and defendant.

- The limitation period is usually 3 years from the date of the accident or the 'date of knowledge'.

- For fatal accidents, the limitation period is usually 3 years from the date of death. However, different limitation periods can apply to different defendants.

- The limitation period does not start to run until a child reaches the age of 18 or until a protected party ceases to be a protected party.

- If the limitation period is missed, the court has a discretion to disregard the limitation period under section 33 of the Limitation Act 1989.

- Strict time limits may apply in relation to accidents involving ships, vessels and aircraft. At the end of a 2-year period the action can be extinguished.

- The 2-year period relating to aircraft applies to hot air balloons and also to passengers embarking and disembarking the aircraft.

- Limitation periods for accidents that happen abroad may be governed by the limitation period in the country where the accident happened.

3 Damages and Interest

The purpose of damages in a personal injury case is to put the claimant in the position he or she would have been had the accident not occurred.

There are usually two elements to a claim for damages:

(a) The claim for the injury itself, ie damages for pain suffering and loss of amenity. The court has to put a financial value on the effect of the injuries.

(b) The financial losses that the injury has caused. This includes damage to items caused in the accident and financial losses and expenditure; and losses which the claimant has suffered or will suffer in the future.

3.1 Damages for pain and suffering

The court will give a value to the pain and suffering the claimant has suffered. This part of the award covers both past and future, physical and mental pain and suffering resulting from the injuries and necessary treatment for them. Such awards were originally assessed by juries but the task now falls to judges who will determine the appropriate amount by considering the awards that have been made in (broadly) comparable cases. These comparable cases are not precedents; the correct approach is for the judge to take judicial notice of other awards (*Waldon v War Office* [1956] 1 WLR 54, CA).

The amounts awarded for pain and suffering and loss of amenity increase over the years as the value of money falls. It is therefore important to approach reported case law with caution and to ensure that the figure awarded is adjusted to represent its contemporary value taking inflation into account.

3.1.1 Judicial Studies Board Guidelines

The most useful starting point is the Judicial Studies Board *Guidelines for the Assessment of General Damages in Personal Injury Cases* (Oxford University Press, 10th edn, 2010) (JSB Guidelines). The JSB Guidelines do not set the rates for awards but attempt to reflect the awards that have been made for specific injuries. In the vast majority of cases the courts will use the Guidelines as a *starting point* for the assessment of damages.

3.1.2   Damages where there are two injuries

The JSB Guidelines may be difficult to apply when the claimant has suffered a number of distinct injuries. The correct approach in these cases is for the court to take into account the amount that would be awarded for each distinct injury but, thereafter, to take an 'overview' of the overall effect of the injuries (*Brown v Woodall* [1995] PIQR 56).

3.2   Damages for financial loss

The object of damages is to put the claimant back in the position he or she would have been had the accident not occurred. The claimant will have to set out, in clear and specific terms, the financial losses he or she has suffered. These include:

*   items damaged in the accident, eg clothing;

*   loss of earnings;

*   any expenses incurred in caring for the claimant;

*   transport costs;

*   aids and appliances.

3.3   Damages for past loss

These cover earnings already lost at the date of trial and expenses resulting from the accident which have already been incurred at that date.

3.3.1   Expenses in connection with a damaged vehicle

These include, for example, the loss of a no claims bonus, towing charges, any reduction in the value of the car despite repair and the cost of alternative transport either hired or public.

3.3.2   Loss of clothing, etc

A claim for damaged clothing can be made. This is assessed on the basis of the value of the clothing at the date of the accident and not the cost of replacing it.

3.3.3   Past loss of earnings

This covers the claimant's net loss from the date of the accident to the date of the trial. In the usual case of a claimant in regular salaried employment, it can be calculated by obtaining details of the claimant's earnings for the 26 weeks before the accident (to allow for variations due to illness, holidays, etc) net of tax and national insurance, and multiplying this by the number of weeks off work.

The claimant should add any pay rises, bonuses and commission which would have been earned. If the claimant is self-employed, he or she must produce accounts for the last few years and expert evidence from accountants may be needed to establish the extent of the loss.

Loss of other fringe benefits, such as free board and lodging or free use of a car, should be added, as should loss of opportunities, for example, taking part in a professional sporting fixture (*Mulvaine Joseph* (1968) 112 SJ 927).

3.3.4   Care needs

If the injured person requires care as a result of his or her injuries, the costs of this care can be recovered as a head of damages. Care that is provided gratuitously by relatives can be recovered. A discount will be made to reflect the fact that tax and National Insurance will not be paid on the sums received (*Housecroft v Burnett* [1986] 1 All ER 332). The sums recovered are paid to the claimant who then holds it on trust for the person who provided the care (*Hunt v Severs* [1994] PIQR Q60). If payment has been made for care, then the claimant should claim the sums actually paid which should be recovered (provided they are reasonable). Where it is the defendant who is providing the care gratuitously, a claim cannot be made for that care (*Hunt v Severs*). Claims for care are not confined to cases where there have been serious injuries (*Giambrone v Sunworld Holidays* [2004] EWCA Civ 158). However, where a claimant has become seriously injured, the care claim can be considerable and may be the highest element of the case, with the need for full-time professional carers, case managers and accommodation for the carers themselves.

3.3.5   Travel to and from hospital and/or medical treatment

Medical treatment costs include National Health Service (NHS) charges, for example, for prescriptions and spectacles, or the cost of private treatment since there is no obligation to use NHS facilities (section 2(4) of the Law Reform (Personal Injuries) Act 1948). Many medical insurers have clauses in their policies which require a claimant to recover the costs of treatment from the negligent defendant.

3.4   Damages for future loss

3.4.1   Future loss of earnings

If the claimant cannot work as a result of the injuries, then the future loss of earnings can be claimed as damages. Similarly, if the claimant's earnings have been reduced as a result, this reduction of earnings may be claimed. The claimant must establish the annual loss (known as the 'multiplicand') and consider the number of years over which this loss occurs ('the multiplier'). The multiplier is not necessarily the number of years of future loss. Instead, it is discounted to take into account the fact that the claimant receives an immediate lump sum which is not earned over a number of years. The multiplier is further discounted to take account of 'contingencies' such as unemployment, redundancy and mortality. Detailed guidance as to appropriate multipliers and applying contingencies can be found in the Government Actuary's Department Actuarial Tables (also referred to as the Ogden Tables), a copy of which can be downloaded from the Government Actuary's Department website, www.gad.gov.uk/Knowledge_Centre/Ogden.html. In assessing future losses, the court will not take into account wage increases arising from future inflation. It will, however, take into account matters such as promotion and advancements in a career.

3.4.2   Loss of pension

The claimant's inability to work, or reduction of earnings, may lead to a loss or reduction of pension. This loss can be claimed as a head of damages (*Auty v National Coal Board* [1985] 1 All ER 930).

3.4.3   Medical expenses

There is no duty on the claimant to use the NHS (section 2(4) of the Law Reform (Personal Injuries) Act 1948); however, the court has to be satisfied that the medical costs will be incurred, that they are reasonable and that they arise as a result of the injuries caused by the defendant's negligence or breach of duty. The cost of future treatment has to be calculated and, if applicable, put on an annual basis with an appropriate multiplier. The cost of travel to medical treatment may also be claimed.

3.5   Travel expenses

Increased travel expenses which arise as a result of the injury can be claimed. Details of motor expenses can be obtained from motoring organisations such as the AA or RAC (*Goldfinch v Scannell* [1993] PIQR Q143). Where specialised transport is required it may be necessary to obtain expert evidence on the costs (*Woodrup v Nichol* [1993] PIQR Q104).

3.6   Disability in the labour market

This covers the situation where instead of, or in addition to, any current loss of earnings, the claimant has been put at a disadvantage on the labour market by the injury, which may cause the claimant to lose his or her job more readily than an able-bodied employee and, as a result, the claimant may find it harder to get another job, or such a well-paid job. The leading case is *Smith v Manchester* Corp (1974) 17 KIR 1, CA. The amount of such awards is always uncertain and can vary from a nominal amount to substantial awards of 2 years' loss of earnings or more, depending on the evidence.

The latest edition of the Ogden Tables (see para 3.4.1) contains a calculation for disability in the labour market/loss of earning capacity. This is only relevant if the claimant is 'disabled' in the strict sense set out in the Disability Discrimination Act 1995.

3.6.1   *Blamires* awards

In cases where the court finds that there will be loss of earnings in the future but that there are too many uncertainties and difficulties to give a definite calculation, then it can take a 'broad brush' approach and award a lump sum (*Blamires v South Cumbria Health Authority* [1993] PIQR Q1). This sum is distinct from an award for a disability in the labour market (*Ronan v Sainsbury's Supermarkets Ltd* [2006] EWCA Civ 1074).

3.6.2   Loss of congenial employment

If the injuries mean that a claimant cannot continue in a job that he or she enjoys, the court can make an award to compensate him or her for this loss (*Hale v London Underground* [1993] PIQR Q30).

3.7   Specialist needs

3.7.1   Care needs

Where there are ongoing care needs it may be necessary to obtain a report from a care expert. The claimant may need assistance on the issue, of the amount of care required, the cost of such care, the additional costs of employing and housing carers, and contingencies for holiday cover. Further consideration will need to be given as to whether a case manager is needed to oversee and assist the claimant's care. It cannot be assumed that care that has been provided gratuitously in the past will continue. Future care needs also to include the inability of the claimant to carry out housework.

3.7.2   Special living accommodation

If the claimant's injuries mean that he or she requires specialised accommodation, these costs can be recovered (in part). The court takes into account the fact that the claimant is acquiring a capital asset and, as a result, capital and mortgage costs are not recoverable (*Roberts v Johnstone* [1989] QB 878). The calculation is complex and is based on the difference in price between the old and new home. Damages are awarded for the loss of use of the capital invested in the new home. The court will award 2.5% per annum multiplied by the relevant multiplier. It is necessary, therefore, to work out the difference in capital costs and to know the relevant multiplier.

In addition, the claimant can claim costs 'thrown away', such as the cost of moving and the additional costs of running the home, as well as carrying out adaptations. Again, the difference in capital costs must be calculated and the appropriate multiplier applied.

3.7.3   Aids and appliances

An injured claimant may not wish to move home but, instead, requires a special toilet, shower or stair lift within the home. Items such as wheelchairs, hoists and orthopaedic beds may be required. In a serious case it is prudent to obtain a report from an occupational therapist. It is important to take into account both the capital costs and the annual costs of upkeep and replacement.

3.8   Provisional damages and periodical payments

3.8.1   Purpose of provisional damages

Normally, only one award of damages can be made. If the claimant's condition later changes, he or she may have been under (or over) compensated. The court will try to take account of such possibilities in fixing its award, but often the parties will seek to delay settling the case until the prognosis is clear. Other procedures for reducing delay in providing compensation for the claimant include interim payments of damages (see para 6.7.2) and trying the issues of liability and quantum separately. The new provisional damages procedure is designed to deal with situations where there is a chance that the claimant will develop some serious disease or suffer some serious deterioration in physical or mental condition (section 32A of the Supreme Court Act 1981 and section 51 of the County Courts Act 1984).

3.8.2   When are provisional damages appropriate?

The reference to 'a chance' of developing a serious disease or deterioration in section 32A implies that something less than the balance of probabilities is sufficient. Most head injuries, for example, carry some risk of epilepsy, clearly a serious deterioration. In *Willson v Ministry* of Defence [1991] 1 All ER 638, a provisional damages claim was refused in a case where the claimant would suffer from osteoarthritis deterioration. It was also said that the courts were concerned with a measurable rather than a fanciful chance.

3.8.3   Provisional damages procedure

(a)   Claimant specifically pleads provisional damages.

(b)   No judgment in default can now be entered.

(c)   Defendant may request further information in respect of possible deterioration.

(d)   Defendant may make written offer to submit to award of provisional damages – similar in effect to payment into court.

(e)   Court makes order for provisional damages after trial or consent summons. Possible deterioration/disease and period for application for further award must be stated.

(f)   Claimant lodges medical report and other documents at court.

(g)   If deterioration occurs, claimant within relevant period gives 3 months' notice to defendant and defendant's insurers of intention to seek further award/extension of period and, within 21 days of end of 3 months, issues and serves summons for directions.

(h)   Directions complied with.

(i)   Court grants/refuses further award.

3.9   Damages payable by instalments (periodical payments)

3.9.1   Purpose of scheme

Damages awarded by the court are usually payable immediately. However, it may be beneficial to the claimant, particularly one who is severely disabled, to receive payment from the defendant by instalments. This has advantages to a claimant because he or she can be certain that the payments (for instance for future care) will be paid throughout his or her lifetime. The payments are linked to an appropriate index and thus the claimant is protected against the effects of future inflation. There can also be advantages to the defendant in that there is no danger of 'overpayment' of damages, particularly if there are issues in relation to the life-expectancy of the claimant. Payments, for instance for future care, will cease when the claimant dies.

3.9.2   Duty of the court

The court has a statutory obligation to consider making an order for periodical payments in all cases where there is a claim for future pecuniary loss (section 2(1)(b) of the Courts Act 2003). The Act and its associated Regulations take care to ensure that continuity of payment under an order is reasonably secure. There are specific provisions against the periodical payments being assigned or charged. There are also provisions to protect the claimant's position should he or she become bankrupt.

A court can make a periodical payments order at trial regardless of the wishes of the parties. However, prior to trial, the parties are still free to settle the case on the basis which they see as best.

The exception to this is when court approval is required in the case of protected persons or minors. Civil Procedure Rules 1998 (SI 1998/3132) (CPR) rule 41.7 and section 2(1)(b) of the Courts Act 2003 state that the court must consider a periodical payments order and will probably not approve any offer if it considers that a periodical payments order should be made.

3.9.3   Procedure

CPR rule 41.5(1) states that, in a personal injury claim, each party in its statement of case may state whether it considers periodical payments or a lump sum to be the more appropriate form for all or part of an award for damages. Where such a statement is given, the party must provide particulars of the circumstances which are relied upon. This is not a mandatory obligation. However, if the parties do not make a statement the court may order one party to make such a statement. If the court thinks that the statement of case provides insufficient particulars, it can order a party to provide such further particulars as it considers appropriate.

CPR rule 41.6 states that the court *shall* consider and indicate to the parties as soon as practicable whether periodical payments are or a lump sum is likely to be the more appropriate form for all or part of an award of damages. CPR rule 41.7 states that when considering whether a lump sum payment or periodical payments is/are likely to be the more appropriate form, the court shall have regard to 'all the circumstances of the case and in particular the form of award which best meets the claimant's needs, having regard to the factors set out in the practice direction'.

3.9.4   Ensuring security for claimant

Section 2(3) of the Damages Act 1996 states that a court may not make an order for periodical payments unless satisfied that the continuity of payment under the order is reasonably secure.

Section 2(4) states that the continuity of payment is reasonably secure if:

(a)   it is protected by a guarantee given under section 6 of or the Schedule to the Act; or

(b)   it is protected by a scheme under section 231 of the Financial Services and Markets Act 2000; or

(c)   the source of payment is a government or health service body.

It has been held that periodical payments made by the MIB are reasonably secure (*Thacker v Steeples & MIB*, 16 May 2005, unreported, Cox J, QBD).

3.9.5   Variable orders

It is possible for the court to make an order for periodical payments which allows a variation if there is a deterioration or an improvement in the claimant's condition.

3.10   Deductions in calculating damages

3.10.1 Income tax and other deductions from earnings

Damages and interest for personal injuries are not taxable when received by the claimant. Accordingly, in recoupment cases, income tax at the highest rate applicable to the claimant is deducted when calculating the past and future loss of earnings (*BTC v Gourley* [1956] AC 185). Further, the claimant must give credit for income tax rebates and the receipt of a tax 'holiday', that is, non-payment of tax for a period on the claimant's return to work (*Brayson v Wilmot-Breedon*, 1 November 1976, unreported; Kemp & Kemp, *The Quantum of Damages* (looseleaf, Sweet & Maxwell), para 12-020).

National insurance contributions that would have been made must also be deducted, as must compulsory superannuation contributions.

3.10.2 Items not deducted

Where a claimant has received assistance from friends, relatives or gratuitous payments, these are not deducted. Similarly, where the claimant receives insurance payments which cover the injury or losses, this does not reduce the amount to be paid by the defendant. In certain circumstances, a claimant may include the money paid out by the insurer in its claim against the defendant, for instance, the cost of vehicle repair or payments covered by health insurance. Before an action is settled, it is prudent for the claimant's representative to check that an insurer does not wish to recover its outlay.

3.10.3 Benefit recovery

Benefit recovery is governed by the Social Security (Recovery of Benefits) Act 1997 (1997 Act). Benefits are recovered by the Compensation Recovery Unit (CRU). The primary intention is to affect all payments of damages for personal injury by requiring the defendant to investigate, before damages are paid, whether social security benefits listed in the statute have been paid to the claimant over the same period of time as that to which the damages relate. Thus benefit recovery may be made against a damages award no matter what its size.

3.10.4 Relevant period

Section 3 of the 1997 Act defines the period during which benefits may be recovered:

(a)   in the case of an accident, the period begins on the day after the accident;

(b)   in the case of a disease, the period begins on the day on which the first claim for benefit is made.

The period for recovery of benefit ends on the occurrence of one of three cut-off dates:

(a) the day when final compensation is paid – this is accepted by the CRU as being the date on which the cheque leaves the compensator's office;

(b) 5 years after the day the recovery period began;

(c) the day it is agreed that an earlier compensation payment finally discharged liability. Thus, the cut-off date is the date of the payment of the sum awarded (*Mitchell v Laing* (1998) *The Times*, 28 January) meaning that if the decision is appealed, the recovery period will continue until the payment of the sum awarded. The *Mitchell* rule does not, however, apply where there has been a payment into court – in such cases, the period for recovery of benefit ends on the day the payment was made, provided that the claimant accepted it within 21 days of receiving notice of it.

3.10.5 Benefits equivalent to heads of damage

The basic aim of the 1997 Act is that there should be a like-for-like deduction – benefits should only be deducted if they duplicate the award of damages by being paid for purposes which are encompassed in the corresponding head of damage. The heads of damage and the corresponding benefits are listed in Schedule 2 to the 1997 Act.

The Act divides the heads of damages against which benefits can be recovered into three sections:

(a) loss of earnings;

(b) loss of mobility;

(c) cost of care.

No benefit can be deducted from certain heads of damage, notably from compensation for pain, suffering and loss of amenity (PLSA). Thus, in extreme cases, the injured person will get some compensation and his award cannot be reduced to nothing. It should also be noted that the 1997 Act requires the compensator to reimburse the state for all recoverable benefits received, even if they cannot be offset fully against the damages.

The benefits which can be set off against certain heads of damages are set out in Schedule 2 to the 1997 Act.

SCHEDULE 2

Calculation of Compensation Payment

(1)	(2)
Head of compensation	*Benefit*
1 Compensation for earnings lost during the relevant period	. . .
	Disablement pension payable under section 103 of the 1992 Act
	[Employment and support allowance]
	Incapacity benefit
	Income support
	Invalidity pension and allowance
	Jobseeker's allowance
	Reduced earnings allowance
	Severe disablement allowance
	Sickness benefit
	Statutory sick pay
	Unemployability supplement
	Unemployment benefit
2 Compensation for cost of care incurred during the relevant period	Attendance allowance
	Care component of disability living allowance
	Disablement pension increase payable under section 104 or 105 of the 1992 Act
3 Compensation for loss of mobility during the relevant period	Mobility allowance
	Mobility component of disability living allowance

3.10.6 How the recoupment system works

By section 23(1) of the 1997 Act, when compensators receive a claim for compensation they must give the Secretary of State certain information about it within 14 days of receiving the claim, as regulated by the Social Security (Recovery of Benefits) Regulations 1997 (SI 1997/2205). This is done by completing and returning Form CRU 1.

Compensators are required to inform the CRU of the following:

(a)   the full name and address of the injured person;

(b)   the injured person's date of birth and National Insurance number;

(c)   the date of the accident or injury;

(d)   the nature of the accident or disease;

(e)   details of the injured person's employment (if the date of the injury or diagnosis of disease was before 6 April 1994).

The CRU will acknowledge receipt of notification of a claim by sending to the compensator Form CRU 4. This form must be used again when the case is about to be settled, as it is the form on which application must be made for a certificate of recoverable benefit which governs the amount of benefit required to be repaid.

3.10.7 Obtaining certificate of recoverable benefit

Before an action is settled, a payment is made into court or payment is made under a judgment, the defendant obtains a certificate of recoverable benefit from the Department of Social Security's (DSS) CRU. The certificate will detail the amount of the relevant benefits paid to the claimant and the defendant pays this amount direct to the DSS and the balance to the victim or into court as the case may be.

3.11   Interest on damages

3.11.1 Purpose of awarding interest

Interest is meant to compensate the claimant for having to wait for the money. Therefore, if the loss has not yet been incurred, no interest is claimable.

3.11.2 Awarding interest

Interest is payable on past losses to compensate the claimant for being deprived of his or her money. The claim for interest must be pleaded in the particulars of claim.

3.11.3 Guidelines on awarding interest

The Supreme Courts Act 1981 and the County Courts Act 1984 leave the period and rate of interest to the discretion of the court. The courts have laid down the following guidelines to cover most cases, though the judge has a discretion not to follow them in appropriate cases. In particular, if one party is guilty of gross delay, the court may increase or reduce the interest rate and/or alter the period for which it is allowed (*Dexter v Courtaulds* [1984] 1 WLR 372).

The guidelines are:

(a)   Special damages carry interest at half the average of the special investment account rates for the period from the date of the accident to the date of the trial (*Pickett v British Rail Engineering* [1980] AC 136).

(b)   Damages for future loss of earnings and future expenses carry no interest since they have not yet been incurred.

(c)   Damages for pain and suffering and loss of amenities normally carry interest at 2% from the date of the service of the claim form to the date of the trial (*Wright v British Railways Board* [1983] 2 All ER 698, HL).

(d)   If special damages are incurred immediately after the accident or the sum has crystallized at some point prior to trial, then there is a strong argument that damages should run at the full rate from that date onwards and at half rate up to that date.

(e)   In a fatal accident case, interest should only be awarded on past losses and not on the whole award (*Train v Fletcher* [2008] EWCA Civ 413).

3.12   Key points

- There is a distinct award for the pain and suffering of the claimant. This is assessed by the judge who will consider previous awards of a similar nature and the guidance in the JSB Guidelines.

- The court will also award damages for the financial losses the claimant has suffered, such as loss of earnings, past care, the cost of medical treatment and items damaged in the accident.

- The claimant can recover damages for matters such as future loss of earnings, future care and future housing costs.

- The court can make an award for provisional damages if it possible that the claimant's medical condition will deteriorate in the future.

- Damages are usually paid in one lump sum. However, in appropriate cases, a court can order that the defendant make regular, periodical payments to cover future losses. These payments are index-linked and the court has to be certain that the payments are fully secure.

- Damages are not taxable; as such, awards for loss of earnings are awarded net of the tax and National Insurance that a claimant would normally pay.

- The government will seek to recoup benefit payments paid to the claimant as a result of the injury.

- A court will award interest on past losses.

4 Fatal Accidents

4.1 Liability in fatal accident claims

When a person is killed, a claim can be brought on behalf of his or her estate and/or on behalf of his or her dependants. The principles of negligence and breach of duty discussed above continue to apply. The claimants have to establish that the deceased would have had an action in negligence or breach of duty had he or she not died. The claimants in the personal injury action 'stand in the shoes' of the deceased (*Gray v Barr* [1971] 2 QB 554). It is necessary to prove that the defendant's breach caused the death or made a material contribution towards it. If the deceased was contributorily negligent, then the claim by the estate or dependants can be reduced.

4.2 Claims on behalf of the estate

The claimant's estate can recover reasonable funeral expenses, any special damages the claimant could have claimed, including loss of earnings (if any), from the date of the accident to the date of death, and general damages for PLSA (unless death was instantaneous). There can only be one action, so if the executors or administrators bring an action on behalf of the estate, they must also bring an action on behalf of the dependants.

4.2.1 Claims brought by dependants

If there are no executors or administrators, a claim can be brought by the dependants: see section 2(2) of the Fatal Accidents Act 1976.

4.2.2 Definition of 'dependant'

The statutory definition of 'dependant' is set out in section 1 of the Fatal Accidents Act 1976. A dependant must fall within this definition to be eligible to bring an action. The dependant must be:

(a)   The wife or husband or former wife or husband of the deceased.

(b)   The civil partner or former civil partner of the deceased.

(c)   Any person living in the same household as the deceased immediately before the death and who had been living with the deceased in the same household for at least 2 years before the death and was living as the husband or wife or civil partner of the deceased.

(d)   Any parent or other ascendant of the deceased.

(e)   Any person treated by the deceased as his or her parent.

(f)   Any child or other descendant of the deceased.

(g)   Any person (not being a child of the deceased) treated by the deceased as a child of the family in any marriage or civil partnership that the deceased was a party to.

(h)   Any brother, sister, uncle or aunt, or their children.

4.2.3   Dependency claims

The fact that a person comes within the statutory definition of dependant does not automatically entitle him or her to bring an action. A dependant must show that he or she has suffered a financial loss or had a reasonable expectation of benefit. The claimant does not have to prove definitively that there is a financial loss; a court can assess the claim on a probability basis (*Davies v Taylor* [1974] AC 207):

(a)   The dependant must show that he or she has suffered a loss (*Yelland v Powell Duffryn Associated Collieries Ltd (No 2)* [1941] 1 KB 519).

(b)   The dependant must show that he or she was receiving benefits from the deceased. This does not have to be a direct financial benefit; it will be enough if the deceased was providing services, eg housework, car servicing or other services which have a financial value.

(c)   A dependent may claim if he or she can show a reasonable expectation of future benefit (see eg *Welsh Ambulance Service Trust v Williams* [2008] EWCA Civ 71 at [31]).

(d)   The court must value the loss suffered by the dependants. It will look at the deceased's earnings, the amount that he or she spent on the dependants and what amount was likely to have been spent in the future. The services provided by a mother, carer or partner can be quantified and damages awarded on that basis (*Bordin v St Mary's NHS Trust* [2000] Lloyd's Rep Med 287).

(e) When assessing a dependant's claim, the court will also take into account the amount the deceased would have spent on him- or herself. Where the deceased and his or her wife, husband or civil partner were living together at the time of death, one third of their joint income will be assessed as having been spent by the deceased on him- or herself; if the couple have dependent children, then that figure is 25% (*Harris v Empress Motors* [1983] 3 All ER 561).

(f) In a fatal accident case, the multiplier runs from the date of death (*Cookson v Knowles* [1979] AC 556). There have been suggestions in the Ogden Tables (see para 3.4.1) and by the Law Commission that this should be changed; however, the courts have consistently confirmed that *Cookson* remains good law (*White v ESAB (UK) Ltd* [2002] PIQR P26 and *MS v ATH* [2002] EWCA Civ 792).

(g) The court is not just concerned with income. Matters such as fringe benefits, services provided and gifts can be part of a proper award.

(h) When the deceased made his or her living off capital it was appropriate to award damages based on the costs of hiring a businessman of appropriate stature to run the business (*Cape O'Loughlin v Cape Distribution Ltd* [2001] EWCA Civ 178, [2001] PIQR Q8). Similarly, the fact that a family took over the deceased's business and continued to run it successfully did not prevent the court awarding damages on a similar basis (*Welsh Ambulance Services v Williams* [2008] EWCA Civ 71).

4.3   Matters which must be disregarded

Any benefit accruing to the estate or dependants as a result of the deceased's death is disregarded when the court is assessing damages. Therefore, any insurance policies, pension payments or similar awards are disregarded. Similarly, where a child's mother died and his or her step-mother proved to be a much better carer and provider, this was a matter that was to be disregarded under section 4 of the Fatal Accidents Act 1976 (*Stanley v Siddique* [1991] 2 WLR 459).

4.4   Bereavement damages

A limited class of people are entitled to bereavement damages of £11,800 upon the death: see section 1A(2) of the Fatal Accidents Act 1976. These are the wife, husband or civil partner of the deceased or the parents of a child who died under the age of 18. If the child's parents are unmarried, the father cannot claim bereavement damages. A former wife, husband or civil partner and cohabitees cannot recover bereavement damage. If the person entitled to the bereavement payment dies before the trial or settlement, the payment does not survive for the benefit of his or her estate: see section 1A of the Law Reform (Miscellaneous Provisions) Act 1934.

4.5   Funeral expenses

Reasonable funeral expenses can be recovered by the estate or the dependants if it/they has/have paid the expenses. These can include the costs of a tombstone but not a memorial to the deceased (*Gammell v Wilson* [1982] AC 27).

4.6   Apportionment

If any of the dependants are children or protected parties, then the court will have to apportion any damages awarded or approve and apportion any sums that relate to the dependant(s). Generally, apportionment is made on a fairly robust basis and takes into account that it is usually a surviving parent who is caring for the remaining children (*R v Criminal Injuries Compensation Board, ex parte Barrett* [1994] PIQR Q44).

4.7   Interest

Damages from the date of death to the date of the trial carry interest. Bereavement damages carry interest at the full rate and there is a strong argument that all losses incurred immediately after the death should carry interest at the full rate. Damages for future loss from the date of the trial carry no interest (*A Train and Sons Ltd v Maxina Emma Fletcher* [2008] EWCA Civ 413).

4.8   Key points

* A claimant in a fatal accidents claim 'stands in the shoes of the deceased' so far as liability is concerned.

* A claim can be brought on behalf of the estate and on behalf of the dependants.

- To be a dependant, a claimant must come within the statutory definition of dependant and have a 'reasonable expectation of benefit' if the deceased person had lived.

- Any benefits arising to the estate or dependants as a result of the death are disregarded in the calculation of fatal accident damages.

- Bereavement damages are payable only to a limited class of relatives.

- Funeral expenses can be recovered.

- In cases involving child dependants or protected parties, the court will apportion the damages.

- Interest in fatal accident claims is paid only on past losses.

5   Financing the Case

5.1   General principles

Both claimants and defendants should consider at the outset how the litigation will be financed.

This necessarily entails an understanding of the general principles as to the award of legal fees (known as 'costs') and of legal help and its alternatives.

This chapter deals with the general principles relating to costs in personal injury litigation. The particular rules relating to costs under the Road Traffic Accident Protocol are discussed in Chapter 6.

5.2   Conditional fee agreements

The conditional fee agreement is now the usual funding basis for personal injury cases. A conditional fee agreement is an arrangement which means that the claimant's solicitor takes the case on the basis that if the claimant wins, he or she will be allowed to charge a success fee, but no fee at all if the claimant loses. The solicitor will be able to charge up to 100% of normal rates. The rules permit the recovery of success fee and insurance premiums from the other side, so removing the need to take part of the client's damages. If the case is lost, the claimant remains liable to pay the defendant's costs. It is usually advisable for the claimant to take out an insurance policy.

5.2.1   Success fees

The solicitor needs to have in place a clear risk assessment procedure for taking on conditional fee agreement cases or face the prospect of financial loss. Solicitors must decide whether the risk is worth taking on and what level the success fee should be. To calculate the success fee, an uplift should be calculated and applied to the costs. In *Gallery v Gray* (2000) TLR, 18 July, the Court of Appeal held that a firm of solicitors taking an 'overview' in simple road traffic accidents and assessing the risk from the outset of instructions was entitled to put forward a mark up of 20%. Success fees in road traffic, accidents at work and industrial disease cases are subject to set rates: see paras 5.10–5.12.

5.2.2   Information to be obtained from and given to the client before conditional fee agreement is made

Before a conditional fee agreement is made, the solicitor should inform the client of certain key matters and, if necessary, provide further information or advice about those matters.

The matters are:

(a)   the circumstances in which a client may be liable to pay the costs of the legal representative;

(b)   the circumstances in which the client may seek assessment of the fees, and the procedure for doing so;

(c)   whether the solicitor considers that the client's risk of incurring liability for costs in respect of the proceedings is insured against in an existing contract of insurance;

(d)   whether other methods of financing the case are available and, if so, how they apply to the client;

(e)   whether the solicitor considers that any particular method of financing any or all of the costs is appropriate and, if he or she considers that a contract of insurance is appropriate, or recommends a particular contract, provide the reasons for doing so and whether the solicitor has an interest in doing so.

Equally important, the solicitor must check whether or not the client has pre-existing insurance which could cover the proceedings. In *Sarwar v Alam* [2001] EWCA Civ 1401, the Court of Appeal held that there was a duty on a solicitor to invite a client, by means of a standard form letter, to bring to the first interview any relevant motor and household insurance policy, as well as any legal insurance policy the client may have. Further, if the injured person was a passenger, the solicitor should attempt to obtain a copy of the driver's insurance policy to assess whether or not it carried legal insurance. The solicitor was not under a duty to go on a 'treasure hunt' and a careful assessment had to be made of whether any policy was suitable for the action. It was suggested that in small cases (that is, less than £5,000) pre-existing policies would normally be satisfactory.

5.2.3   Contents of conditional fee agreements

A conditional fee agreement must be in writing and must state the percentage increase which is being sought. The Law Society has produced a model conditional fee agreement and guidance leaflet for clients, 'Your clients – your business', available from The Law Society website, www.lawsociety.org.uk.

5.2.4   Notifying the other side

Any party who wishes to claim an additional liability in respect of a funding arrangement, that is, a conditional fee agreement, must give the other party information about the claim if he or she is to recover the additional liability, although it is not necessary to specify the amount of additional liability separately nor to state how it is to be calculated until it falls to be assessed. The claimant must give notice of the following matters (see Form N251 at para 5.15.1). That he or she has:

(a)   entered into a conditional fee agreement which provides for a success fee, stating the date of the agreement, identifying the claim to which it relates and including Part 20 claims, if any;

(b)   taken out an insurance policy to which section 29 of the Access to Justice Act 1999 applies, stating the name of the insurer, the date of the policy and identifying the claim to which it relates;

(c)   made an arrangement with a body which is prescribed for the purpose of section 30 of the Act, stating the name of the body, the date and terms of the undertaking it has given and identifying the claim to which it relates.

Where a party has entered into more than one funding arrangement, such as a conditional fee agreement and an insurance policy, a single notice containing the information set out in Form N251 (see para 5.15.1) may contain the information about both of them. Where a claimant has entered into a conditional fee agreement before starting proceedings to which it relates, he or she must file the notice when he or she issues the claim form.

It is essential that the claimant's lawyer informs the defendant of the existence of a conditional fee agreement as soon as possible. This should be done in the initial letter of claim.

Some defendants will ask claimants for *details* of the risk assessment, mark up and premium paid. This is not information to which the defendant is entitled. Claimants should refuse to disclose this information since it could harm their case and their negotiating position.

5.2.5   Notification by the defendant

A defendant who has entered into a funding arrangement before filing any document must provide information to the court by filing notice with his or her first document. A first document may be an acknowledgment of service, a defence or any other document.

5.2.6   Change of situation

CPR rule 44.15 imposes a duty on a party to give notice of change if the information he or she has previously given is no longer accurate. To comply, he or she must file and serve a notice in Form N251 (see para 5.15.1). Further notification must be given if the insurance cover is cancelled or if new cover is taken out with a different insurer.

5.3   Funding clinical negligence claims

A wider range of public funding is currently available for clinical negligence cases. Funding can only be made for claims where the solicitor has a contract with the Legal Services Commission in clinical negligence, which usually means membership of a specialist panel of the Law Society or Action for Victims of Medical Accidents. The general funding code applies, but if mediation is offered and rejected by the claimant, it must be justified or funding may be refused or discontinued. If the value of the claim is not likely to exceed £10,000, investigative help may be refused if pursuing the NHS complaints procedure is more appropriate for the client. If an application is made for a claim worth less than £10,000, the solicitor must justify why the complaints procedure is not appropriate. Investigative help may only be granted where investigative work is required to determine the prospects of success. The solicitor should be satisfied on the basis of the limited information available that there is a real possibility that a negligent act or omission has caused the *claimant's* injury. A formal investigative definition will be given with the initial certificate.

5.4   Alternatives to Community Legal Service funding

5.4.1   Legal expenses insurance

The client may have a specific legal expenses policy. More likely, the client will have cover under a more general policy such as house contents, a motor policy or a small boat or pet insurance policy. The insurers may, however, have the right to nominate solicitors to deal with claims covered by the policy, so the wording of the particular policy should be checked. In *Sarwar v Alam* [2001] EWCA Civ 1401, the Court of Appeal held that there was a specific duty on solicitors to enquire about the existence of such policies. However, in that case, it was held that the policy in question was not suitable and the claimant could recover the cost of the after-the-event legal expenses policy from the defendant.

5.4.2 Trade unions

These may well provide legal assistance for industrial injury claims, again normally conditional on using a particular firm of solicitors. Many trade union cases will be funded under collective conditional fee agreements.

5.5 Liability for costs between the parties

It is essential to consider the issues of costs at the outset of a case. The CPR require the successful party to serve with the bill of costs a 'short but adequate written explanation of any agreement between the client and solicitor which affects the costs claimed'; a copy of any such agreement must be attached to the court copy of the bill. It is vital that such an agreement is executed at the start of the case.

The court has the power to, and will normally, make a summary assessment of costs immediately after trial in fast track cases and may do so in multi-track cases. It will generally assess the costs of interlocutory hearings during the course of the claim. At the allocation questionnaire and the listing questionnaire stage (for details of the allocation questionnaire, see para 11.1.2; the listing questionnaire (Form N170) is at para 11.8.4, the solicitor is expected to give an accurate assessment of costs expended to date and an estimate of costs of proceeding with the litigation to its conclusion (see Form N260 at para 5.15.2).

5.5.1 The court's discretion

The award of costs is within the discretion of the court. Normally, the loser will be ordered to pay the costs of the winner, although in some cases these will not be the costs of the whole proceedings. By CPR rule 44.3(4) and (5), in deciding what order as to costs is to be made, the court is required to take into account matters such as the conduct of the parties (including whether pre-action protocols have been complied with) and the issue of proportionality – that is to say the amount of costs incurred in relation to the value of the claim. The court has a complete discretion as to whether costs are payable and by whom, the amount of the award and when it is to be paid.

A fundamental aim of the new rules is to discourage what the court will view as unreasonable and tardy behaviour by imposing costs penalties. An overly adversarial approach risks adverse costs orders, whether or not that party wins the claim. Furthermore, although the general rule that an unsuccessful party will be ordered to pay the costs of the successful party still applies, the CPR encourage the court to consider a range of alternative orders.

5.5.2   The amount of costs

The amount of costs payable by one party to another is limited to the costs of the action (*Re Gibson's Settlement Trusts* [1981] Ch 179) and these will not include all the work done for the client. The basis on which costs between the parties is ordered is the standard basis, that is, a reasonable amount in respect of all costs reasonably incurred, the benefit of the doubt on questions of reasonableness being given to the *paying* and not the receiving party.

The more generous indemnity basis will only be awarded in exceptional cases, for example, where the court disapproves strongly of the way the paying party has conducted the case. Costs will be allowed, unless they are an unreasonable amount or have been incurred unreasonably; any doubt being resolved in favour of the *receiving* party. These rules remain under the CPR but are reformed by rule 44.4(1) which provides that the court will not in either case allow costs which have been unreasonably incurred, or unreasonable in amount.

CPR rule 35.4(4) gives the court an express power to limit the amount a party may recover with regard to expert's fees.

In deciding the amount of costs, the factors to be taken into account are laid down in CPR rule 44.5(3) and include:

(a)   the conduct of the parties before and during the proceedings;

(b)   the efforts made to resolve the dispute (if any);

(c)   the value of the claim;

(d)   the importance of the matter;

(e)   the complexity, time and skill involved in the case;

(f)   the area in which the work was conducted.

5.5.3   Interim applications

These are applications to the court made after the proceedings have begun and before final judgment. In a routine case, the usual order will be costs in the case, that is, the recipient of the costs of that application will be the party who wins the trial. However, where the application has been made necessary by the unreasonable attitude of the other side in, for example, not giving proper discovery or inadequate particulars of a pleading, then the solicitor should ask the court to award costs to the client in any event.

The general rule is that, wherever a 'costs in any event' order is made at the conclusion of an interim application, the court should make a summary assessment of costs unless there is good reason not to do so. The assessed costs will be payable within 14 days of the order unless otherwise stated. A summary assessment cannot be made against a party under a legal disability (a child or a protected party).

5.5.4   Part 36 offers to settle

These are set out in detail in Chapter 10. CPR Part 36 sets out the procedure that the parties can use to put pressure on other parties to settle the claim. A party can make a Part 36 offer to settle. If the opposing party rejects the offer and the party making the offer does better than or equals the offer he or she has made, then there are penalties. Where a defendant makes an offer that has not been beaten at trial, the claimant will normally have to pay the costs of both sides from 21 days after the date of the offer. Where a claimant makes an offer and he or she receives a better award at trial, the defendant will have to pay increased interest and indemnity costs running from 21 days after the offer.

Where there are split trials, a party can make an offer to accept liability up to a specified proportion of the amount fixed by the court. Finally, a defendant may offer to submit to an award of provisional damages.

5.5.5   Where there are several claimants or defendants

Two or more successful claimants with the same interest will normally recover only the costs of one set of solicitors and counsel, unless the court thinks that separate representation was justified. If the claimants fail, then the court will apportion their liability for the defendant's costs.

Co-defendants may be separately represented, but the extra costs will only be allowed if the court thinks that separate representation was required (*Harbin v Masterman* [1896] 1 Ch 351). When the claimant has reasonably joined several defendants as parties to the proceedings, costs are allowed against them all, provided the claimant succeeds against them all.

If the claimant succeeds against only some, he or she will generally have to pay the costs of the successful defendant, but they can be recovered from the unsuccessful defendant (*Bullock v London General Omnibus Co* [1907] 1 KB 264). However, if the claimant is on legal aid, or is of limited means, the losing defendant may be ordered to pay the costs of the successful defendant direct (*Sanderson v Blyth Theatre Co* [1903] 2 KB 533).

5.5.6   Costs against the solicitor

Note that the court has the power to award costs against the party's legal representatives who are guilty of misconduct or neglect in the conduct of the proceedings. However, this power cannot be exercised summarily. The court has to follow a detailed procedure. A notice to show cause must state precisely what the lawyers are said to have done wrong and they must be given a chance to respond: see CPR rule 48.7.

Alternatively, or in addition, the court can order the solicitor's bill to be disallowed in whole or part.

5.6   Types of costs in personal injury cases

5.6.1   Assessed costs

These are scrutinised and approved by the court. This will be the usual position in personal injury cases in the absence of agreement.

5.6.2   Agreed costs

It is common for the parties to agree costs to save the expense of a detailed assessment.

5.6.3   Client's right to seek assessment of costs

Where the court has assessed solicitor/own client costs either summarily or by way of detailed assessment, the client may apply for assessment either of the base costs, or the success fee, or both. Base costs are assessed under the indemnity principle. The court has the power to reduce the success fee where it considers it to be disproportionate, having regard to all the relevant factors as they would have reasonably appeared to the solicitor to be when the conditional fee agreement was entered into. Relevant factors include the disadvantage caused by the lack of any payments on account, whether the agreement contains a cap on the proportion of damages which can be subject to the success fee and the extent to which the solicitor is liable to pay disbursements.

5.7   Costs under the fast track

There are fixed trial costs for the fast track depending on the value of the claim. The value is determined by the amount recovered (excluding interest, costs and contributory negligence) if the claimant is recovering costs and the amount claimed if the defendant is recovering costs:

Less than £3,000	£485
Between £3,000 and £10,000	£690
Between £10,000 and £15,000	£1,035
More than £15,000	£1,650

If the court thinks that it was necessary for a legal representative to attend to assist the advocate, the court can award an additional £345.

Note that these are trial costs only. The court will assess the costs of preparing for trial, which are not subject to a fixed costs regime.

5.8   Costs between solicitor and client

5.8.1   Liability for costs

The client, unless in receipt of funding from the Legal Services Commission, is contractually bound to pay the solicitor's proper costs, whether or not the solicitor wins the case and whether or not an order for costs is obtained against the opponent. The position in relation to claims brought under a conditional fee agreement is ambiguous since the indemnity principles still apply. Further, it is not possible to agree to be paid a proportion of any damages recovered, since this would amount to a contingency fee. The client's liability is to pay solicitor and client costs. It is for the client to show that items or amounts claimed are unreasonable, and unusual steps will be deemed reasonable if the client approved them. The solicitor should, therefore, seek the client's written approval for major items of expenditure and warn the client in the case of unusual items (for example, a mad accident simulation by a consulting automobile engineer) that the cost may not be recovered from the opponent.

5.8.2   Duties to the client

The solicitor should inform the client as accurately as possible of the likely cost before starting proceedings, giving warning of the difficulties of doing so and explaining when and what items of expenditure are likely to arise. The solicitor should also regularly report the costs position to the client, who should be told that a limit may be imposed on the costs to be incurred on his or her behalf. Finally, it should be pointed out not only that, if the case is lost, the client is likely to have to pay the other side's costs, but also that, even if the case is won, the solicitor will be charging solicitor and client costs, yet is likely to recover only standard basis costs from the other side.

5.9   Fixed recoverable costs in road traffic accidents

The intention of the rule is to provide an agreed scheme of recovery which is certain and easily calculated. It may sometimes over reward and other times it may under reward, but it aims to provide fairness on the whole. Many road traffic cases will be subject to the Road Traffic Accident Protocol: see Chapter 6.

5.9.1   Fixed costs

The fixed costs are £800, plus 20% of the damages agreed up to £5,000 and 15% of the damages agreed between £5,000 and £10,000.

If the claimant lives or works, or instructs a solicitor who practises in London (including Bromley, Croydon, Dartford, Gravesend and Uxbridge), then an additional 12.5% of this total amount can be recovered. In essence, there is a 'London allowance'.

5.9.2   Disbursements

The cost of obtaining the following can be recovered:

(a)   medical records;

(b)   a medical report;

(c)   a police report;

(d)   an engineer's report;

(e)   a search of the records of the Driver Vehicle Licensing Authority;

(f)   an insurance premium.

Further, if one or more of the claimants was a child or protected party, then the following may also be recoverable:

(a)   fees payable for instructing counsel;

(b)   court fees.

There is also a discretionary head for any other disbursements which have arisen due to a 'particular feature' of the dispute.

5.9.3   Success fee

The claimant may recover a success fee if he or she has entered into a conditional fee agreement. However, this success fee is stipulated at 12.5% of the total fixed recoverable costs.

5.10   Fixed percentage increase in road traffic accident claims conducted under conditional fee agreement

In road traffic accident cases there is a prescribed success fee where the increase depends on the stage of litigation at which the case resolves.

CPR Part 45 allows for a percentage increase in road traffic accident claims. This is the amount of a legal representative's fee that can be increased where there is a conditional fee agreement which has a success fee.

The percentage increase cannot be used in:

(a)   costs only proceedings;

(b)   small track claims;

(c)   accidents before 6 October 2003.

5.10.1 Solicitor's fees

In relation to the solicitor's fees, there can be a 100% increase where the claim concludes at trial, or a 12.5% increase where the claim concludes before a trial has commenced or the dispute is settled before a claim is issued.

5.10.2 Counsel's fees

For counsel's fees, there can be a 100% increase where the claim concludes at trial.

If the claim has been allocated to the fast track, counsel can receive:

(a)   a 50% increase if the claim concludes 14 days or less before the trial;

(b)   a 12.5% increase if the claim concludes more than 14 days before the trial.

If the claim has been allocated to the multi track, counsel can receive:

(a)   a 75% increase if the claim concludes 21 days or less before the trial;

(b)   a 12.5% increase if the claim concludes more than 21 days before the trial.

Further, counsel can only receive a 12.5% increase when:

(a)   the claim has been issued but has not been allocated a track;

(b)   the dispute is settled before a claim is issued (costs-only proceedings).

5.10.3 Percentage increase greater than 12.5%

Where the fixed percentage increase is 12.5%, a party may apply for a greater or lesser percentage increase if:

(a)   damages are £500,000 or more are awarded; or

(b)   damages would have been £500,000 or more if there had not been a finding of contributory negligence.

In such circumstances, the court can then either assess the percentage increase or make an order for the percentage increase to be assessed.

In such circumstances, if the percentage increase is assessed as greater than 20% or less than 7.5%, the new decided percentage increase shall be allowed.

If the percentage increase is assessed as no greater than 20% and no less than 7.5%, the percentage increase shall be 12.5%, and the costs of the application and assessment shall be paid by the applicant.

5.11   Fixed percentage increase in employer's liability claims where claim conducted under conditional fee agreement

5.11.1 Scope

There are fixed percentages for the success fee in employer's liability cases where the claim is conducted under a conditional fee agreement.

This applies where:

(a)   there is a dispute between an employer and employee;

(b)   the employee sustained a bodily injury in the course of his or her employment;

(c)   the claimant had entered into a conditional fee agreement.

It does not apply where:

(a)   the dispute relates to a disease;

(b)   the injury was sustained before 1 October 2004;

(c)   it arises from a road traffic accident;

(d)   it would be a small claims track claim.

5.11.2 Solicitor's fees

In relation to solicitor's fee, there can be a 100% percentage increase where the claim concludes at trial, or 25% where the claim concludes before a trial has commenced or the dispute settled before a claim is issued.

5.11.3 Counsel's fees

For counsel's fees, there can be a 100% increase where the claim concludes at trial.

If the claim has been allocated to the fast track, counsel can receive:

(a)   a 50% increase if the claim concludes 14 days or less before the trial;

(b)   a 25% increase if the claim concludes more than 14 days before the trial.

If the claim has been allocated to the multi track:

(a)   a 75% increase if the claim concludes 21 days or less before the trial;

(b)   a 25% increase if the claim concludes more than 21 days before the trial.

Further, counsel can only receive a 25% increase when:

(a)   the claim has been issued but has not been allocated a track;

(b)   the dispute is settled before a claim is issued (costs-only proceedings).

5.11.4 Percentage increases of more than 25%

Where the fixed percentage increase is 25%, a party may apply for a greater or lesser percentage increase if:

(a)   damages of £500,000 or more are awarded; or

(b)   damages would have been £500,000 or more if there had not been a finding of contributory negligence.

In such circumstances, the court can then either assess the percentage increase or make an order for the percentage increase to be assessed.

In such circumstances, if the percentage increase is assessed as greater than 40% or less than 15%, the new decided percentage increase shall be allowed.

If the percentage increase is assessed as no greater than 40% and no less than 15%, the percentage increase shall be 25%, and the costs of the application and assessment shall be paid by the applicant.

5.12 Fixed recoverable success fees in employer's liability disease claims

5.12.1 Scope

CPR Part 45 applies where:

(a) the dispute is between an employee and his or her employer;

(b) the dispute relates to a disease with which the employee has been diagnosed;

(c) it is alleged that the disease was contracted as a consequence of an employer's alleged breach of duty, in the course of the employment;

(d) the claimant had entered into a conditional fee agreement;

(e) the letter of claim was issued after 1 October 2005.

5.12.2 Types of claim

Three types of claim are relevant here:

(a) Type A claim – this is a disease or physical injury alleged to have been caused by asbestos, ie absestosis, mesothelioma, bilateral pleural thickening, pleural plaques.

(b) Type B claim – this is a claim relating to:

   (i) a psychiatric injury alleged to have been caused by work-related stress;

   (ii) a work-related upper limb disorder which is alleged to have been caused by psychical stress or strain (excluding hand/arm vibration injuries), ie repetitive strain injury/work-related upper limb disorders or carpal tunnel syndrome caused by repetitive strain injury occupational stress.

(c) Type C claim – this is a claim relating to a disease that does not fall within Type A or Type B.

5.12.3 Solicitor's fees

In relation to solicitor's fee, there can be a 100% percentage increase where the claim concludes at trial.

Where the claim concludes before a trial has commenced or the dispute settled before a claim is issued, the following increases apply:

(a)   Type A claims – 27.5%;

(b)   Type B claims – 100%;

(c)   Type C claims – 62.5%.

5.12.4 Counsel's fees

For counsel's fees, there can be a 100% increase where the claim concludes at trial.

If the claim has been allocated to the fast track:

(a)   where the claim concludes 14 days or less before the trial the following increases apply:

    (i)   Type A claims – 50%;

    (ii)   Type B claims – 100%;

    (iii)   Type C claims – 62.5%.

(b)   where the claim concludes more than 14 days before the trial or before such a date has been fixed the following increases apply:

    (i)   Type A claims – 27.5%;

    (ii)   Type B claims – 100%;

    (iii)   Type C claims – 62.5%.

If the claim has been allocated to the multi track:

(a)   where the claim concludes 14 days or less before the trial the following increases apply:

    (i)   Type A claims – 75%;

    (ii)   Type B claims – 100%;

    (iii)   Type C claims – 75%.

(b)   where the claim concludes more than 14 days before the trial or before such a date is fixed the following increases apply:

    (i)   Type A claims – 27.5%;

    (ii)   Type B claims – 100%;

    (iii)   Type C claims – 62.5%.

5.12.5 Percentage increase

A party may apply for a greater or lesser percentage increase if:

(a)   damages of £250,000 or more are awarded; or

(b)   damages would have been £250,000 or more if there had not been a finding of contributory negligence.

In such circumstances, the court can then either assess the percentage increase or make an order for the percentage increase to be assessed. However, the percentage increase cannot be varied where the case concludes at trial.

5.13 Costs and the Motor Insurers' Bureau and Criminal Injuries Compensation Authority

5.13.1 Motor Insurers' Bureau untraced driver's agreement

The MIB will pay reasonable costs under the uninsured driver's agreement on the normal basis; however, under the untraced driver's agreement, the MIB will pay £150 profit costs plus VAT and reasonable disbursements, plus a further £75 for each extra claimant.

5.13.2 Criminal Injuries Compensation Authority

The CICA will not pay applicants' legal costs, but may pay the expenses of the applicant and any witnesses.

5.14 Key points

• Conditional fee agreements are now a common way of conducting personal injury litigation.

• Investigations must be made as to alternatives before a claimant enters into a conditional fee agreement.

• It is essential that the other side is notified of the existence of a conditional fee agreement as soon as possible, preferably as soon as the agreement is entered into.

- The success fee in a conditional fee agreement is determined by an assessment of the risks involved. However, there are fixed success fees in road traffic, employer's liability and industrial disease cases.

- Fixed recoverable costs are in place in relation to road traffic accidents.

5.15   Forms

The following forms are reproduced in full below:

5.15.1 Notice of funding of case or claim (N251)

Notice of funding of case or claim

Notice of funding by means of a conditional fee agreement, insurance policy or undertaking given by a prescribed body should be given to the court and all other parties to the case:
- on commencement of proceedings
- on filing an acknowledgment of service, defence or other first document; and
- at any later time that such an arrangement is entered into, changed or terminated.

Click here to reset form	Click here to print form

In the

The court office is open between 10 am and 4 pm Monday to Friday. When writing to the court, please address forms or letters to the Court Manager and quote the claim number.

Claim No.	
Claimant (include Ref.)	
Defendant (include Ref.)	

Take notice that in respect of

☐ all claims herein

☐ the following claims

☐ the case of *(specify name of party)*

[is now][was] being funded by:

(Please tick those boxes which apply)

☐ a conditional fee agreement
Dated

which provides for a success fee

☐ an insurance policy issued on
Date   Policy no.

Name and address of insurer

Level of cover

Are the insurance premiums staged?

☐ Yes ☐ No

If Yes, at which point is an increased premium payable

☐ an undertaking given on
Date

by

Name of prescribed body

in the following terms

The funding of the case has now changed:

☐ the above funding has now ceased

☐ the conditional fee agreement has been terminated

☐ a conditional fee agreement
Dated

which provides for a success fee has been entered into;

☐ an insurance policy
Date

has been cancelled

☐ an insurance policy has been issued on
Date   Policy no.

Name and address of insurer

continued over the page ➡

Level of cover

Are the insurance premiums staged?

☐ Yes ☐ No

If Yes, at which point is an increased
premium payable

☐ an undertaking given on

Date

has been terminated

☐ an undertaking has been given on

Date

Name of prescribed body

in the following terms

Signed

Solicitor for the (claimant) (defendant)
(Part 20 defendant) (respondent) (appellant)

Dated

Click here to print form

5.15.2 Statement of costs (summary assessment) (N260)

Click here to reset form	Click here to print form

**Statement of Costs
(summary assessment)**

In the	
	Court

Judge/Master

Case Reference	

Case Title

[Party]'s Statement of Costs for the hearing on *(date)*   **(interim application/fast track trial)**

Description of fee earners*

(a) *(name) (grade) (hourly rate claimed)*	
(b) *(name) (grade) (hourly rate claimed)*	
(c) *(name) (grade) (hourly rate claimed)*	
(d) *(name) (grade) (hourly rate claimed)*	

Attendances on *(party)*

(a) *(number)*	hours at £	£
(b) *(number)*	hours at £	£
(c) *(number)*	hours at £	£
(d) *(number)*	hours at £	£

Attendances on opponents

(a) *(number)*	hours at £	£
(b) *(number)*	hours at £	£
(c) *(number)*	hours at £	£
(d) *(number)*	hours at £	£

Attendance on others

(a) *(number)*	hours at £	£
(b) *(number)*	hours at £	£
(c) *(number)*	hours at £	£
(d) *(number)*	hours at £	£

Site inspections etc

(a) *(number)*	hours at £	£
(b) *(number)*	hours at £	£
(c) *(number)*	hours at £	£
(d) *(number)*	hours at £	£

Work done on negotiations

(a) *(number)* [ ] hours at £ [ ] £ [ ]

(b) *(number)* [ ] hours at £ [ ] £ [ ]

(c) *(number)* [ ] hours at £ [ ] £ [ ]

(d) *(number)* [ ] hours at £ [ ] £ [ ]

Other work, not covered above

(a) *(number)* [ ] hours at £ [ ] £ [ ]

(b) *(number)* [ ] hours at £ [ ] £ [ ]

(c) *(number)* [ ] hours at £ [ ] £ [ ]

(d) *(number)* [ ] hours at £ [ ] £ [ ]

Work done on documents

(a) *(number)* [ ] hours at £ [ ] £ [ ]

(b) *(number)* [ ] hours at £ [ ] £ [ ]

(c) *(number)* [ ] hours at £ [ ] £ [ ]

(d) *(number)* [ ] hours at £ [ ] £ [ ]

Attendance at hearing

(a) *(number)* [ ] hours at £ [ ] £ [ ]

(b) *(number)* [ ] hours at £ [ ] £ [ ]

(c) *(number)* [ ] hours at £ [ ] £ [ ]

(d) *(number)* [ ] hours at £ [ ] £ [ ]

(a) *(number)* [ ] hours travel and waiting time £ [ ] £ [ ]

(b) *(number)* [ ] hours travel and waiting time £ [ ] £ [ ]

(c) *(number)* [ ] hours travel and waiting time £ [ ] £ [ ]

(d) *(number)* [ ] hours travel and waiting time £ [ ] £ [ ]

Sub Total £ [ ]

Brought forward £ [ ]

Counsel's fees *(name) (year of call)* [ ]

       Fee for [advice/conference/documents]   £ [ ]

       Fee for hearing   £ [ ]

Other expenses

       [court fees]   £ [ ]

       Others   £ [ ]
       (give brief description)

       Total   £ [ ]

       Amount of VAT claimed

          on solicitors and counsel's fees   £ [ ]

          on other expenses   £ [ ]

       Grand Total £ [ ]

The costs stated above do not exceed the costs which the *(party)* is liable to pay in respect of the work which this statement covers. Counsel's fees and other expenses have been incurred in the amounts stated above and will be paid to the persons stated.

(party) [ ]

Dated [ ]   Signed [ ]

Name of firm of solicitors [partner] for the *(party)* [ ]

* 4 grades of fee earner are suggested:

(A) Solicitors with over eight years post qualification experience including at least eight years litigation experience.

(B) Solicitors and legal executives with over four years post qualification experience including at least four years litigation experience.

(C) Other solicitors and legal executives and fee earners of equivalent experience.

(D) Trainee solicitors, para legals and other fee earners.

"Legal Executive" means a Fellow of the Institute of Legal Executives. Those who are not Fellows of the Institute are not entitled to call themselves legal executives and in principle are therefore not entitled to the same hourly rate as a legal executive.

In respect of each fee earner communications should be treated as attendances and routine communications should be claimed at one tenth of the hourly rate.

Click here to print form

6 Road Traffic Accident Protocol

On 30 April 2010 a new procedure came into place which is designed to speed up the procedure in 'small value' road traffic claims. A key element of such claims is the use of technology with the entire pre-action process taking place by use of an electronic communication known as the 'portal'.

The process applies to road traffic claims where:

(a) the value of the claim is between £1,000 and £10,000 and contains an element of personal injury;

(b) the accident occurred in England and Wales;

(c) the accident occurred after the implementation date – 30 April 2010.

There are excluded categories: see para 6.2.

6.1 Rights to act for a claimant under the new process

Only solicitors are permitted to recover the fixed recoverable costs under the new process. In practical terms, this confines representation to solicitors. Any other body or organisation that acts for claimants will not recover costs

6.1.1 Claimants in person

Claimants in person are discouraged and insurers are actively encouraged to refer a claimant to a solicitor. However, claimants in person will be able to deal directly with the defendant/insurer without using the process.

Where an offer is made to a claimant in person through the process, he or she must be informed of the set time period in which he or she can accept or reject the offer and that, if the offer is accepted, he or she can make no further claim. Claimants in person must also be informed of their right to seek legal independent advice from a solicitor, Citizens Advice Bureau, law centre or trade union.

6.2   Excluded categories

There are a number of claims which are excluded from the process. The pre-existing pre-action protocols and costs regimes continue to apply to:

(a)   claims that fall within the small claims limit, ie where less than £1,000 compensation is recoverable for PLSA;

(b)   claims involving employers' liability and/or public liability;

(c)   MIB claims for untraced drivers;

(d)   claims where the claimant or defendant is deceased (and note that it does not appear that this death has to be a result of the accident);

(e)   claims where the claimant is bankrupt;

(f)   claims where the claimant or defendant is a protected party.

(A 'protected party' is defined in CPR rule 21.2 as a party or intended party who lacks capacity to conduct the proceedings.)

The procedural aspects of these matters were introduced into the Rules by Practice Direction 8B and the Pre-Action Protocol for Low Value Personal Injury Claims in Road Traffic Accidents (Road Traffic Accident Protocol).

6.3   Determining the value of the claim

For the purpose of deciding whether a claim falls within the process, the central element is the overall value of the personal injury aspect of the claim.

(a)   the claim will need to include a minimum of £1,000 compensation for PLSA;

(b)   furthermore, the overall value of the claim must be no more than £10,000 on a full liability basis when including general and special damages but excluding interest.

6.3.1   Vehicular damage and car hire costs

The costs of repairing a vehicle and car hire costs are *excluded* for the purpose of determining whether or not the claim comes within the process. However, despite being excluded from the issue of valuation, car hire and vehicle damage costs *can* be recovered as an element of special damage within the process.

In some, if not many, cases the costs of repair and car hire can greatly exceed the personal injury aspect of the claim. Despite this, these claims will still come within the process if the claim is less than £10,000.

6.3.2 Disbursements are not part of the value of the claim

Paragraphs 4.1(3) and 1.1(5) of the Protocol make it clear that the value of the claim does not include disbursements incurred as part of the claims process, for instance a medical report.

6.3.3 Initial valuation of the claims

Paragraph 9.1 of the Protocol recognises that there will be claims where the value of the claim is assessed as having reasonable prospects of exceeding £1,000 for PLSA.

6.3.4 Claim valued at too high a level

Where claims are valued at too high a level:

(a) the fixed recoverable costs for Stage 1 will be paid on all claims;

(b) Stage 2 fixed recoverable costs will be paid and reasonable disbursements will be met where there was a reasonable prospect of exceeding £1,000 PLSA;

(c) the claim will exit the process and the defendant must notify the claimant that the claim is valued at less than £1,000 where it becomes clear in Stage 2 that the value of the claim was less than £1,000 PLSA.

(See paras 6.5 et seq for an explanation of the stages.)

6.3.5 Value of claim exceeds £10,000

In cases where it was initially thought that the claim would be less than £10,000, but it becomes clear that this sum is likely to be exceeded:

(a) the claim will exit the process;

(b) the claimant must notify the defendant that the claim is valued at more than £10,000;

(c) the court can limit the costs awarded to the claimant up to the maximum of the fixed recoverable costs applicable to the new process where the claim is later found by the court to have unreasonably exited the process.

6.4   General principles

Once a claim has left the process it may not re-enter. However, as we have seen above, if the court finds that the claim has left the process unreasonably, a court can confine the award of costs to those sums which could be recovered under the process.

6.5   Procedure

The key part of the initial procedure is that all communication between the parties takes place via the portal. The address for electronic communication can be found at www.rtapiclaimsprocess.org.uk.

The procedure is broken down into three stages:

(a)   Stage 1 – essentially the notification stage where the parties exchange information;

(b)   Stage 2 – the negotiation stage;

(c)   Stage 3 – the litigation stage.

6.6   Stage 1 – notification of claim and insurer's response

6.6.1   Claim notification form

A claimant must complete the claim notification form (CNF) (see Form RTA 1 at para 6.11.1).

Every box on the CNF, except the question of how the claim is referred, is mandatory. Some boxes will need to be noted as not applicable. The only optional field is where the referrer of the work is asked to be identified (to prevent fraud).

The aim of the CNF is to ensure that the defendant is provided with all the information he or she will need to make a decision as to how to progress the claim (ie whether or not to accept liability). For this reason a detailed checklist is attached.

6.6.2   Checklist of information needed for claim notification form

General information

- Date sent.
- Solicitor's name.
- Solicitor's address.
- Name of case handler.
- Direct telephone number of case handler.
- Email address of case handler.
- Reference number.
- Defendant's full name.
- Defendant's vehicle registration number.
- Insurer reference.
- Referral source (optional).

Information about claimant

- Claimant's full name.
- Claimant's address and postcode.
- Claimant's date of birth.
- Is claimant a child?
- Claimant's National Insurance number (or explanation as to why there is no number).
- Claimant's occupation.
- Claimant's vehicle registration number.

Details of injury

- Accident date.
- Details of injury.
- Brief description of injury.
- Has claimant had any time off work? If so, how long?
- Is claimant still off work?

- Has claimant sought any medical attention?
- Date when claimant first sought medical attention.
- Did claimant attend hospital?
- Details of the hospital.
- Was claimant detained overnight in hospital?
- If so, how long was claimant in hospital?
- Was claimant wearing a seatbelt?
- Has there been any recommendation for rehabilitation?
- If so, details of rehabilitation.
- Is solicitor aware of any rehabilitation needs that arise out of the accident?

Vehicle damage

- Was claimant's vehicle damaged in the accident?
- Details of insurance cover for the vehicle.
- Is the claim for repairs proceeding through the insurer?
- Is the claim for repairs proceeding through another company?
- Details of company repairing.
- Current position of repairs.
- Is insurer required to organise repairs and/or inspection of the vehicle?
- If yes, full details of the vehicle location.
- If claimant is not responsible for the repair element of the claim, full details of the owner of the vehicle.

Use of alternative vehicle

- Does claimant require the use of an alternative vehicle?
- Has claimant been provided with the use of an alternative vehicle?
- Is the hire of the vehicle still ongoing?
- Name and address of provider.
- Details of vehicle being provided: make, model and engine size.

- Does claimant require insurer to provide him with an alternative vehicle?
- Class of vehicle required and claimant's name, address and telephone number.

Passengers and other details

- How many passengers were in the vehicle?
- What was position of claimant, ie was he or she the driver, owner of vehicle but not driving, a passenger, a cyclist?
- If claimant was a passenger, details of the driver of the vehicle unless the driver is the defendant.
- Make and model of vehicle, registration number, insurance company name and address and policy number.
- If claimant was a passenger, details of the driver of the vehicle unless the driver is the defendant.
- Name, address and postcode of passengers, make and model of vehicle, vehicle registration number, insurance company name and address, policy number.

Details of accident

- Time of accident.
- Place of accident, street name, town, city.
- Weather conditions.
- Road conditions.
- Description of accident.
- Brief description of accident, including approximate speed of the vehicles and details of the areas of vehicle damage.
- Was the incident reported to the police? If so, name and address of police station, name of reporting officer and reference number.

Defendant's details

- If defendant driver was uninsured, are details known?
- Defendant's full name, address, registration number of vehicle, vehicle make and model, description of defendant, approximate age

of defendant, sex of defendant and description of how defendant's details were obtained.

- Other party details, eg other driver or witnesses, full name, address, vehicle registration number, make and model, insurance company name, address and policy number.

- If action involves a bus or coach, description of driver, description of vehicle including route number, direction of travel, type and livery of vehicle. Is evidence of travel available (ie bus ticket). If not, why not?

- Who does claimant believe was responsible for the accident and why?

- If another party is potentially responsible, provide details.

Funding

- Has claimant entered into a conditional fee agreement?

- If so, date conditional fee agreement entered into.

- Name and address of insurance company, policy number, policy date, level of cover, whether insurance premiums are staged, point at which an increased premium is payable.

- If a membership organisation is meeting costs, name of organisation and date of agreement.

- If an MIB claim, would claimant like to be considered for free legal insurance?

Other information

- Other relevant information.

6.6.3   Stage 1 procedure

As soon as the claimant's solicitor has all the information required to complete the CNF it will be sent electronically via the electronic portal to the defendant's insurer.

The CNF must be sent to the appropriate electronic address. The claimant's solicitor or the claimant will sign the statement of truth on the CNF. It should not be sent until the claimant's signature is obtained or the claimant's solicitor has signed.

The insurer will then send a receipt or acknowledgment. At the same time a modified version of the form will be sent to the defendant (certain personal details are omitted).

If a mandatory field on the CNF is not completed so as to enable a decision on liability to be made within 15 days, the claim may exit the process and the fixed recoverable costs of the process will not apply. If the court subsequently considers that the claimant's solicitor could have obtained the omitted information and that the claim should have remained in the process, the claimant's recoverable costs will be limited to the fixed recoverable costs associated with the process.

When the CNF has been correctly completed, the insurer will have 15 business days to respond. The response is set out in the response section of the CNF and sent electronically to the defendant's solicitor. The 15-day period will begin on the business day after the claim notification was sent by the claimant's solicitor. See the checklist for the insurer's response at para 6.6.6.

During the 15-day period, the claimant will carry out no further work. *There will be no extensions on the time period for decisions on liability.*

Where the defendant's insurer admits liability within 15 business days but alleges contributory negligence (other than failure to wear a seatbelt), the claim may leave the process. The defendant's insurer will set out the reasons for alleging contributory negligence in the response section of the CNF and send this electronically to the claimant's solicitor. Fixed recoverable costs for Stage 1 will be payable.

Where there is no response or a denial of liability, the claim leaves the process. Fixed recoverable costs under Stage 1 will not be paid. When the insurer denies liability it should be made clear whether the whole claim is denied or certain parts and, if so, which parts. The reasons for the denial of liability should be stated on the response section of the CNF.

Where the claimant's rehabilitation needs have not already been met, the need for rehabilitation should be raised, as appropriate. Fields on the CNF allow for rehabilitation, which needs to be considered and addressed in accordance with the Rehabilitation Code as set out in Annex D of the Pre-Action Protocol for Personal Injury Claims (see para 7.12). The Code sets out that rehabilitation should be considered from the outset. Rehabilitation should be available to the claimant whenever the need arises during the process.

When fraud is alleged in Stage 1 or at any later stage in the process, the claim will leave the process and fixed recoverable costs will not be payable.

6.6.4 Motor Insurers' Bureau claims

The MIB has 30 business days to reply to the CNF. The CNF will be emailed to the MIB, which has a dedicated email address for these claims. For details of how to contact the MIB, see Appendix 1. The 30-day period begins on the business day after the claim notification was sent by the claimant solicitor.

The process applies to uninsured cases only (ie where the defendant driver is identified). The CNF lists additional questions in relation to MIB cases.

Claims under the untraced driver's agreement do not follow the system.

Where it is not possible for the claimant to provide the defendant's address, then the claim will not be eligible for the new process. Where the defendant's policy is declared void after the accident, the insurers will continue to handle the claim (in place of the MIB) within the new claims process.

6.6.5   End of Stage 1 payment of fixed recoverable costs

Fixed recoverable costs of £400 will be paid at the end of Stage 1 where liability is admitted (whether or not contributory negligence is alleged).

A 12.5% success fee is also applied to Stage 1 fixed recoverable costs. However, this success fee is only paid at the end of Stage 2, when the case settles.

Payment of these costs will be made within 10 business days from the end of the 15-day period allowed for responding to the CNF (or 30 days for MIB claims).

Where payment of fixed recoverable costs is not made, then the claim will leave the process. If the claim is eventually settled before trial, the maximum the court may award is the fixed costs under CPR Part 45. Where the claim proceeds to trial, the normal CPR costs rules and claims process will apply.

6.6.6   Checklist for insurer response

- In what capacity is insurer acting?

- Does defendant admit that the accident occurred, that it was caused by defendant's breach of duty and caused claimant loss to some extent?

- If liability is not admitted, reasons must be given.

- Is insurer prepared to provide rehabilitation or has this already been given? If so, details of rehabilitation.

- Has insurer instructed a 'mobility provider' (eg temporary replacement for a damaged vehicle? If so, details of provider.

- Has insurer organised repairs or arranged an inspection? If so, details.

- Date of notification.

- Date of response to notification.

- Defendant's insurer details.

- Address.

- Name of claims handler

- Direct telephone number of case handler.

- Email address of case handler.

- Reference number.

6.7   Stage 2 – offers to settle and negotiations

Once the defendant's insurer has admitted liability, the claimant's solicitor should obtain a medical report from a medical expert. The medical expert should use the medical report form provided (see Form RTA 3 at para 6.11.2). No further work should be carried out on the claim until all medical reports have been obtained; there is no time limit for obtaining the reports.

6.7.1   Additional medical reports

Further medical reports should only be obtained on the recommendation of the medical experts writing the reports; for example, where further treatment is needed. If it is clear that an additional medical report is required from a medical expert in a different discipline, then a second report may be obtained without waiting for the recommendation of the medical expert.

6.7.2   Interim payments

An interim payment may be sought where the first medical report identifies the need for a second report. The claimant's solicitor should send the first medical report and an interim settlement pack form (see para 6.7.4) to the insurer. An interim payment of £1,000 should then be made within 10 business days.

If the claimant's solicitor requests the second medical report without the recommendation of the medical expert, then an interim payment cannot be sought.

Where the payment is in excess of £1,000, the interim settlement pack should still be sent with reasons why a payment in excess of £1,000 is required. The defendant then has 10 business days to decide whether to pay the interim payment request by the claimant. If he or she rejects this, the claim will leave the process. An interim payment of £1,000 should be made within 10 business days and the claimant can then issue proceedings to recover the additional amount of the interim payment in the usual way.

6.7.3   Errors

Once the medical report has been received, it should be checked by the claimant for any factual errors. Where such an error is identified, the report should be returned to the expert and amended. The claimant's solicitor should notify the defendant's insurer of the reason for the delay.

6.7.4   Settlement pack

Within 15 days of the medical report being confirmed as correct, the claimant's solicitor should prepare a settlement pack form (see Form RTA 4 at para 6.11.3). This must be sent electronically to the insurers together with the medical report. Any evidence of special damages claimed, along with receipts for disbursements incurred, should also be sent.

The insurer must either accept the claimant's offer or make a counter offer within 15 business days of receiving the settlement pack.

6.7.5   Early end to the process

The claim will leave the Stage 2 process without providing the chance of negotiation where:

(a)   the defendant denies causation; or

(b)   there is an allegation of fraud; or

(c)   there is a failure to respond after the 15-day period.

6.7.6   Counter offers

Counter offers should be made on the settlement pack form. This passes between both parties. The defendant should state why the amount proposed is not agreed. This is to try to encourage settlement by focussing on the areas which are in dispute. If a counter offer is made, there will be 20 business days for negotiation between the parties. This can be extended by agreement between the parties.

6.7.7   Where there is no agreement

Where no agreement to settle has been reached after the 20-day period, a Stage 3 hearing will be held to determine quantum. The claimant's solicitor will prepare a court proceedings pack form (see Form RTA 6 at para 6.11.4). This will include the final offers, and the claimant's and defendant's comments on why each head of damage is in dispute. It should be noted that once this is complete, there will be no further opportunity in Stage 3 to provide new documents or evidence.

6.7.8   Sending the court proceedings pack form

The court proceedings pack form will then be sent to the defendant's insurer electronically, which will then have 5 business days to check the accuracy of the form and make any comments. This should then be returned to the claimant's solicitor electronically. Where the defendant does not return the form, it can be assumed that the defendant has nothing further to add.

6.7.9   Payments at the end of Stage 2

Whether or not there has been an agreement, the defendant will pay the full amount of the defendant's final offer by way of an interim payment. Fixed recoverable costs of £800 must also be paid (these apply to all claims taken under the process from the beginning to the end of Stage 2). These payments will be paid within 10 business days.

Where agreement has not been reached, then if at the hearing the claimant is awarded less than the defendant's interim payment, the insurer may take steps to recover the over-payment.

6.8   Stage 3 – no agreement on quantum

Where quantum cannot be agreed through negotiation, it will be for the court to determine the level of damages to be awarded. The claimant must follow the procedure set out in CPR Practice Direction 8B.

6.8.1   Application to the court

After 10 business days of sending the court proceedings pack form to the insurer, the claimant may make an application to the court. The claim form should state:

(a)   that the claimant has followed the procedure set out in the Road Traffic Accident Protocol;

(b)   the date when the court proceedings pack form was sent to the defendant;

(c)   whether the claimant wants the claim to be determined by the court on the papers or at a Stage 3 hearing;

(d)   the dates which the claimant requests should be avoided; and

(e)   the value of the claim.

6.8.2   Types of hearings

A Stage 3 hearing means a final hearing to determine the amount of damages that remain in dispute between the parties. There is a presumption that there will be a paper hearing unless either party requests an oral hearing or the judge otherwise directs.

6.8.3   Filing at court

The claimant should file at court:

(a)   the claim form;

(b)   medical report(s);

(c)   the court proceedings pack form:

    (i)   Part A;

    (ii)   Part B (lodged in a sealed envelope);

(d)   receipts supporting the claim for special damages;

(e)   disbursements incurred during the process (ie costs of medical reports);

(f)   any notice of funding.

All documents should also have been sent to the defendant and no new documents or evidence should be provided.

6.8.4   Acknowledgement of service

The defendant must file an acknowledgement of service within 14 days of service of the claim form. The acknowledgment of service must state whether the defendant:

(a)   contests the amount of damages claimed;

(b)   contests the making of an order for damages;

(c)   disputes the court's jurisdiction;

(d)   objects to the use of the Stage 3 procedure (if so, reasons must be given);

(e)   wants the claim to be determined by the court on the papers or at a Stage 3 hearing.

6.8.5   Paper hearing

This is a hearing whereby the evidence will be presented on paper, with no oral submissions. If there is a paper hearing, the court will notify parties of its decision with written reasons.

6.9   Recoverable costs

Where the claim concludes at trial and the claimant wins, the claimant's solicitor will be able to recover costs of £250 for paper hearings and £500 for oral hearings. These costs and damages ordered to the claimant will be paid in accordance with the usual CPR provisions, see CPR rule 40.11.

The defendant's solicitor's recoverable costs will be fixed in Stage 3 only. These will be at £250 for paper hearings and £500 for oral hearings.

Where an offer is made and settlement is reached between the issue of the claim and before trial commences, the claimant's solicitor can recover costs of £250. These costs and the damages agreed should be paid within 10 days of settlement being reached.

6.10   Key points

- Road traffic claims with a value of less than £10,000 are subject to the Road Traffic Accident Protocol.

- All initial communications take place by electronic communications via a portal.

- Negotiations, offers and counter offers take place through the portal.

- There are fixed payments of costs which the defendant must make at the end of Stage 1 and Stage 2.

- If the matter cannot be resolved, proceedings are issued using the court proceedings pack form.

6.11 Forms

The following forms are reproduced in full below:

6.11.1 Claim notification form (RTA 1)

Claim notification form (Form RTA1)

Low value personal injury claims in
road traffic accidents(£1,000 - £10,000)

Before filling in this form you are encouraged to seek independent legal advice.

Date sent ☐☐ / ☐☐ / ☐☐☐☐

Items marked with (✱) are optional and the claimant must make a reasonable attempt to complete those boxes.
All other boxes on the form are mandatory and must be completed before being sent.

Are you a litigant in person?   ☐ Yes   ☐ No   *If you are the litigant in person please put your details in the claimant's representative section.*

Claimant's representative - contact details	Defendant's details
Name	Defendant's name
Address	Defendant's address ✱
Postcode ☐☐☐☐ ☐☐☐	Postcode ☐☐☐☐ ☐☐☐
Contact name	Defendant's vehicle registration number
Telephone number	Policy number reference
E-mail address	Insurer name
Reference number	

Referral source ✱
Please state the source from which this claim was referred

© Crown copyright 2010

1

Section A — Claimant's details

☐ Mr.   ☐ Mrs.   ☐ Ms.

☐ Miss   ☐ Other ____

Claimant's name

____

Address

____

Postcode ☐ ☐ ☐ ☐ ☐ ☐ ☐

Date of birth

☐ ☐ / ☐ ☐ / ☐ ☐ ☐ ☐

Is this a child claim? ☐ Yes ☐ No

National Insurance number

☐ ☐ ☐ ☐ ☐ ☐ ☐ ☐ ☐

If the claimant does not have a National Insurance number, please explain why

____

Occupation

____

Claimant's vehicle registration number *(if applicable)*

____

Accident date

☐ ☐ / ☐ ☐ / ☐ ☐ ☐ ☐

Section B — Injury and medical details

1.1   What type of injury was suffered?

☐ Soft tissue   ☐ Bone injury   ☐ Whiplash

☐ Other

Please provide a further brief description of the injury sustained as a result of the incident

____

1.2   Has the claimant had to take any time off work as a result of the injury?

☐ Yes   ☐ No

1.3   Is the claimant still off work?

☐ Yes   ☐ No

If No, how many days in total was the claimant off work?

____

1.4   Has the claimant sought any medical attention?

☐ Yes   ☐ No

If Yes, on what date did they first do so?

☐ ☐ / ☐ ☐ / ☐ ☐ ☐ ☐

this section continues over the page ⇨

2

Section B — Injury and medical details

1.5 Did the claimant attend hospital as a result of
the accident? ☐ Yes ☐ No

If Yes, please provide details of the
hospital(s) attended

If hospital was attended, was the claimant
detained overnight? ☐ Yes ☐ No

If Yes, how many days were they detained?

Section C — Rehabilitation

2.1 Has a medical professional recommended the
claimant should undertake any rehabilitation ☐ Yes ☐ No ☐ Medical professional not seen
such as physiotherapy?

If Yes, please provide brief details of the
rehabilitation treatment recommended and any
treatment provided including name of provider

2.2 Are you aware of any rehabilitation needs that the
claimant has arising out of the accident? ☐ Yes ☐ No

If Yes, please provide full details

3

Section D — Vehicle damage

3.1 Is the claimant claiming damage to their own vehicle?

☐ Yes ☐ No   If No, please go to Section F

3.2 Details of the insurance cover held for the vehicle?

☐ Comprehensive

☐ Third party fire and theft

☐ Third party only

☐ Other (please specify) [   ]

3.3 Is the claim for vehicle damage proceeding through the claimant's insurer?

☐ Yes ☐ No

If No, is the claim for vehicle damage proceeding through an alternative company?

☐ Yes ☐ No

If the claim is proceeding through an alternative company, please provide full details, if known*

[   ]

3.4 Is the vehicle a total loss or likely to be?

☐ Yes ☐ No ☐ Not known

If No, what is the current position with the repairs?

☐ Complete

☐ Authorised

☐ Not yet authorised

☐ Not known

3.5 Do you require the defendant's insurer to organise the repairs and/or inspection of the vehicle?

☐ Yes ☐ No

If Yes, please provide contact details and where the vehicle is located

[   ]

4

Section E — Alternative vehicle provision

(If the claimant has been provided a vehicle by their insurer, please go to Section F)

4.1 Does the claimant require the use of an alternative vehicle? ☐ Yes ☐ No

4.2 Has the claimant been provided with the use of an alternative vehicle? ☐ Yes ☐ No

If Yes, is the hire need still on going? ☐ Yes ☐ No

4.3 If a vehicle has been provided, please give the following details:

Name of provider

Address of provider

Reference

Start date ☐☐ / ☐☐ / ☐☐☐☐

End date ☐☐ / ☐☐ / ☐☐☐☐

Vehicle registration number*

Make*

Model*

Engine size (cc)*

4.4 Do you require the defendant's insurer to provide your client with an alternative vehicle? ☐ Yes ☐ No

If Yes, please provide the following details:

What type of vehicle is required?

Contact name and telephone number

Section F — Accident details

5.1   At the time of the accident the claimant was

☐ The driver
☐ The owner of the vehicle but not driving
☐ A passenger in or on a vehicle owned by someone else
☐ A pedestrian
☐ A cyclist
☐ A motorcyclist
☐ Other (please specify) [   ]

5.2   If the claimant was the driver or passenger, how many occupants were in the claimant's vehicle?

[   ]

5.3   If the claimant was the driver or a passenger, was the claimant wearing a seatbelt?

☐ Yes   ☐ No   ☐ Seatbelt not supplied

5.4   If the claimant was a passenger please provide the details of the driver and the owner of the vehicle in which the claimant was a passenger unless the driver is the defendant:

Driver's name*   [   ]

Address*   [   ]

Postcode [ ][ ][ ][ ] [ ][ ][ ]

If owner not the driver, owner's name*   [   ]

Make and model of vehicle*   [   ]

Vehicle registration number*   [   ]

Insurance company name*   [   ]

Address*   [   ]

Postcode [ ][ ][ ][ ] [ ][ ][ ]

Policy number*   [   ]

6

Section G — Accident time, location and description

6.1 Estimated time of accident (24 hour clock)

6.2 Where did the accident happen?

6.3 Weather and road conditions

Weather conditions   ☐ Sun   ☐ Rain   ☐ Snow   ☐ Ice   ☐ Fog
☐ Other *(please specify)*

Road conditions   ☐ Dry   ☐ Wet   ☐ Snow   ☐ Ice
☐ Mud   ☐ Oil   ☐ Other *(please specify)*

6.4 Please select the most accurate description of the accident circumstances from the list opposite

☐ Claimant vehicle hit by party emerging from side road

☐ Claimant vehicle hit in the rear

☐ Claimant vehicle hit whilst parked

☐ Accident in a car park

☐ Accident on a roundabout

☐ Accident involving vehicles changing lanes

☐ Concertina Collision

☐ Other

this section continues over the page ⇨

7

Section G — Accident time, location and description (continued)

6.5   Please give a brief description of the accident,
       including approximate speeds of all vehicles and
       details of the areas of vehicle damage

6.6   Was the incident reported to the police?   ☐ Yes   ☐ No   ☐ Not known

       If Yes, please provide the following, if known:

                Name and address of police station*

                      Name of Reporting Officer*

                            Reference number*

Section H — MIB Claims - For uninsured cases only

7.1 Details of defendant and vehicle

Full name

Address

Postcode

Vehicle registration number

Make

Model

Colour

7.2 Description of defendant

7.3 Approximate age of defendant

7.4 Sex of defendant   ☐ Male   ☐ Female   ☐ Not known

7.5 How were the defendant's details obtained?

9

Section I — Other party details

8.1 If parties other than the claimant and defendant were involved or there were witnesses please provide their details below:

☐ Not applicable ☐ Witness

☐ Other party (please specify)

8.2

Name

Address

Postcode ☐☐☐ ☐☐☐

Vehicle registration number*

Vehicle make and model*

Insurance company name*

Address*

Postcode ☐☐☐ ☐☐☐

Policy number*

this section continues over the page ⇨

10

Section I — Other party details (continued)

8.3

☐ Witness   ☐ Other party (please specify) [   ]

Name

Address

Postcode [ ][ ][ ] [ ][ ]

Vehicle registration number*

Vehicle make and model*

Insurance company name*

Address*

Policy number*

8.4

☐ Witness   ☐ Other party (please specify) [   ]

Name

Address

Postcode [ ][ ][ ] [ ][ ]

Vehicle registration number*

Vehicle make and model*

Insurance company name*

Address*

Postcode [ ][ ][ ] [ ][ ]

Policy number*

11

Section J — Accidents involving a bus or a coach

9.1 Where the accident involved a bus or a coach, please complete the following:

Driver name and ID number*

Description of the driver*

Description of vehicle, including route number and direction of travel, type, colour and markings of vehicle

Approximate number of passengers on the bus/coach*

9.2 Is evidence of travel available?

☐ Yes ☐ No

If No, please state why not

Section K — Liability

10.1 Why does the claimant believe that the defendant was responsible for the incident?

10.2 If the claimant believes that another party noted in Section I could bear some responsibility, please confirm which*

Section L — Funding

11.1 Has the claimant undertaken a funding arrangement within the meaning of CPR rule 43.2(1)(k)?   ☐ Yes   ☐ No

If Yes, please tick the following boxes that apply

☐ The claimant has entered into a conditional fee agreement in relation to this claim, which provides for a success fee within the meaning of section 58(2) of the Courts and Legal Services Act 1990

Date conditional fee arrangement was entered into   ☐☐ / ☐☐ / ☐☐☐☐

☐ The claimant has taken out an insurance policy to which section 29 of the Access to Justice Act 1999 applies.

Name of insurance company   [   ]

Address of insurance company   [   ]

Policy number   [   ]

Policy date   ☐☐ / ☐☐ / ☐☐☐☐

Level of cover   [   ]

Are the insurance premiums staged?   ☐ Yes   ☐ No

If Yes, at which point is an increased premium payable?   [   ]

☐ The claimant has an agreement with a membership organisation to meet their legal costs.

Name of organisation   [   ]

Date of agreement   ☐☐ / ☐☐ / ☐☐☐☐

☐ Other, please give details   [   ]

For MIB Claims only

11.2 The claimant would like their claim to be considered for free legal expenses insurance   ☐ Yes   ☐ No

13

Section M — Other relevant information*

Section N — Statement of truth

Your personal information will only be disclosed to third parties, where we are obliged or permitted to do so. This includes use for the purpose of claims administration as well as disclosure to third-party managed databases used to help prevent fraud, and to regulatory bodies for the purposes of monitoring and/or enforcing our compliance with any regulatory rules/codes.

Where the claimant is a child the signature below will be by the child's parent or guardian or by the legal representative authorised by them.

☐ I am the claimant's solicitor. The claimant believes that the facts stated in this claim form are true. I am duly authorised by the claimant to sign this statement.

☐ I am the claimant. I believe that the facts stated in this claim form are true.

Signed   **Date**

☐☐ / ☐☐ / ☐☐☐☐

Position or office held
(if signed on behalf of firm or company)

☐ I have retained a signed copy of this form including the statement of truth.

Claim notification form (Form RTA1)
Low value personal injury claims in
road traffic accidents (£1,000 - £10,000)

Insurer response

Capacity

In what capacity is the insurer acting in this case?

- [ ] Insurer in contract
- [ ] RTA Insurer
- [ ] Article 75 Insurer on behalf of MIB
- [ ] MIB
- [ ] Other *(please specify)* _____

Section A — Liability

For MIB claims only

Please select the relevant statement from those opposite

- [ ] The MIB consent to being added to the Stage 3 Procedure as a second defendant.

  The MIB has no authority contractual or otherwise to bind another defendant but subject there to will say that one of the options below applies.

Defendant admits:
Accident occured

Caused by the defendant's breach of duty

Caused some loss to the claimant, the nature and extent of which is not admitted

- [ ] The above are admitted
- [ ] The defendant makes the above admission but the claim will exit the process due to contributory negligence other than failure to wear a seatbelt

If the defendant does not admit liability please provide reasons below

Section B1 — Services provided by the insurer - Rehabilitation

Is the insurer prepared to provide rehabilitation?   Yes   No

Has the insurer provided rehabilitation?   Yes   No

If Yes, please provide full details below

Section B2 — Services provided by the insurer - Alternative vehicle provision

Has the insurer instructed the supply of an
alternative vehicle?   Yes   No

If Yes, please provide full details below

Section B3 — Services provided by the insurer - Repairs/Inspection

Has the insurer organised repairs or arranged an inspection?   ☐ Yes   ☐ No

If Yes, please provide full details below

Section C — Response information

Date of notification   ☐☐/☐☐/☐☐☐☐

Date of response to notification   ☐☐/☐☐/☐☐☐☐

Defendant's date of birth*   ☐☐/☐☐/☐☐☐☐

Defendant's insurer details

Address

Contact name

Telephone number

E-mail address

Reference number

6.11.2 Medical report form (RTA 3)

| Click here to reset form | Click here to print form |

Medical report form (RTA3)
Low value personal injury claims in road traffic accidents (£1,000 to £10,000)

The first report is without notes except where requested by medical experts

Section A — Claimant's details

Claimant's full name

Date of birth

Occupation

Address

Postcode

1.1   Has photo ID been confirmed?

Yes   No

If Yes, what type of photo ID was checked

If No, what other ID was provided

1.2   Age of the claimant at time of accident?

1.3   Date of examination

1.4   Date of report

1.5   Name of instructing solicitors/agency

1

Section B

History

Please give a brief description of the accident, immediate symptoms and treatment. Include a history of treatment, specifying whether the claimant was treated as an in-patient or outpatient where applicable. Detail any improvement or deterioration of symptoms including dates. In the case of injuries/symptoms fully recovered, please specify the date by which there was a full recovery. Whether the claimant has ever experienced symptoms in the injured area prior to the accident and if so give full details including type of injury and date it occured.

Present position reported by claimant

Please detail all ongoing symptoms reported at examination

Section C

Employment position/Education

Please give details of the claimant's employment/education at the time of the accident. Include the dates of any absences, part-time work or light duties undertaken and the nature of any light duties. Set out the claimant's current situation at work/educational establishment including any practical difficulties, symptoms and/or restrictions.

Consequential effects

Please state the impact on other activies such as hobbies, recreations, housework, gardening, travelling, holidays, shopping, sex life. Give details as to the claimants general state of mind.

3

Section D

Past medical history

Please refer to any relevant history based on examination or records as appropriate.
Post accident records should be considered where appropriate.

On examination

Please state your findings on examination including the details of any restrictions arising
from the accident.

4

Section D - continued

Diagnosis opinion and prognosis

Please state your overall opinion of the claimant's position to date dealing with causation and including a prognosis if possible. Set out all reported symptoms and restrictions identified under the claimant's present position. Refer to the claimant's employment/ education position and any impact to the claimants home life. Please detail whether you consider that the claimant has/will make a recovery and to what extent and when this will be reached. Identify if the claimant has any further needs, including but not limited to :
- if further treatment is necessary;
- if time is needed to make a final prognosis;
- if a report is needed from a medical expert of a different discipline; or
- if a follow up report is needed.

5

Section E

Seatbelts

Was the claimant wearing a seatbelt?   ☐ Yes   ☐ No

Does the claimant have an exemption from wearing a seatbelt?   ☐ Yes   ☐ No

If Yes, please state form of exemption

If No, state what extent would each of the claimant's injuries have been prevented all together; have been less severe; or have been unchanged by the claimant's failure to wear a seatbelt?

Section F

Future treatment and rehabilitation

Please give details of any further treatment and/or rehabiliation that the claimant will require.

Section G

Statement of truth

> Civil Procedure Rule 35.3 states that it is the duty of experts to help the court on matters within their expertise. This duty overrides any obligation from whom experts have received instructions or by whom they are paid.

I confirm that I have made clear which facts and matters referred to in this report are within my own knowledge and which are not. Those that are within my own knowledge I confirm to be true. The opinions I have expressed represent my true and complete professional opinions on the matters to which they refer.

Signature

Date

7

6.11.3 Interim settlement pack form and response to interim settlement pack (RTA 4)

Click here to reset form | Click here to print form

Interim Settlement Pack Form and Response to Interim Settlement Pack (Form RTA4)

Low value personal injury claims in road traffic accidents (£1,000 - £10,000)

Claimant's full name

Claimant's representative

Date of notification

Contact details

Company name

Contact name

Telephone number

E-mail address

Reference number

Defendant's full name

Defendant's representative

Date of insurer response

Contact details

Company name

Contact name

Telephone number

E-mail address

Reference number

1

Interim settlement pack and response

Claimant losses to date							Defendant response					
Loss	Claim item being pursued Yes/No/N/A	Evidence attached	Comments	Gross value claimed	% contributory negligence deductions	Net value claimed	Is gross amount agreed?	Comments	Gross value offered	% contributory negligence deductions	Net value offered	Amount in dispute
Policy excess												
Loss of use												
Car hire												
Repair costs												
Fares (taxis, buses, tube, etc.)												
Medical expenses												
Clothing												
Care/Services												
Loss of earnings a) Claimant												
b) Employer												
Other losses												
General damages												
Total heads of net damage claimed to date												

Losses offered to date

CRU deductions

Net value of offer to date

2

Claimant request for interim payment	
Date	Value of interim request

Detail reasons for interim payment request below

Defendant responses to interim payment request	
Date	Value of interim payment agreed

Additional comments below

Statement of truth

☐ I am the claimant's solicitor - The claimant believes that the facts stated in this claim form are true. I am duly authorised by the claimant to sign this statement.

☐ I am the claimant - I believe that the facts stated in this claim form are true.

Signed

Date

Position or office held
(if signed on behalf of firm or company)

☐ I have retained a signed copy of this form including the statement of truth.

6.11.4 Court proceedings pack (Part A) Form (RTA 6)

Click here to reset form | Click here to print form

Court Proceedings Pack (Part A) Form (Form RTA6)
Low value personal injury claims in road traffic accidents (£1,000 - £10,000)

Date of accident

Claimant's full name

Age

Occupation, if any

Defendant's full name

Claimant's representative

Contact details

Company name

Contact name

Telephone number

E-mail address

Reference number

Defendant's representative

Contact details

Company name

Contact name

Telephone number

E-mail address

Reference number

1

Court Proceedings Pack (Part A)

Claimant Losses	Item being pursued Yes/No	Evidence attached	% Interest rate	Claimant Gross value claimed	% contributory negligence deductions	Net value claimed	Comments	Defendant response Gross value offered	% contributory negligence deductions	Net value offered	Comments
Policy excess											
Loss of use											
Car hire											
Repair costs											
Fares - taxis, buses, tube etc.											
Medical expenses											
Clothing											
Care/Services											
Loss of earnings a) Claimant											
b) Employer											
Other losses											
General damages											

CRU benefits received

Up to date CRU Certificate attached

2

Are all disbursements agreed and paid? ☐ Yes ☐ No   If No, please give the following details:

Disbursements disputed	Amount claimed	Amount paid	Reason given by defendant for not paying full disbursement

Has the defendant named a legal representative to accept service of legal proceedings on the defendant's behalf   ☐ Yes   ☐ No

If Yes, please give details of the legal representative

Statement of truth

☐ I am the claimant's solicitor – The claimant believes that the facts stated in this claim form are true. I am duly authorised by the claimant to sign this statement.

☐ I am the claimant – I believe that the facts stated in this claim form are true.

Signed

Date

Position or office held
(if signed on behalf of firm or company)

☐ I have retained a signed copy of this form including the statement of truth.

6.11.5 Court proceedings pack (Part B) Form (RTA 7)

Court Proceedings Pack (Part B) Form (Form RTA 7)
Low value personal injury claims in road traffic accidents (£1,000 - £10,000)

This form should be submitted to the court in a sealed envelope

Date of accident

Claimant's full name

Defendant's full name

Claimant's representative

Defendant's representative

Contact details

Company name

Contact name

Telephone number

E-mail address

Reference number

Contact details

Company name

Contact name

Telephone number

E-mail address

Reference number

Claimant final offer

Judge's award

Defendant final offer

Fixed costs   Stage 1 fixed costs paid ☐   Stage 2 fixed costs paid ☐

Click here to reset form   Click here to print form

4

6.12 Civil Procedure Rules Practice Direction 8B – Pre-Action Protocol for Low Value Personal Injury Claims in Road Traffic Accidents – Stage 3 Procedure

(This Practice Direction supplements CPR rule 8.1(6).)

Contents of this Practice Direction

General

1.1

This Practice Direction sets out the procedure ('the Stage 3 Procedure') for a claim where –

(1)   the parties –

    (a)   have followed the Pre-Action Protocol for Low Value Personal Injury Claims in Road Traffic Accidents ('the RTA Protocol'); but

    (b)   are unable to agree the amount of damages payable at the end of Stage 2 of the RTA Protocol;

(2)

    (a)   the claimant is a child;

    (b)   a settlement has been agreed by the parties at the end of Stage 2 of the RTA Protocol; and

    (c)   the approval of the court is required in relation to the settlement in accordance with rule 21.10(2); or

(3)   compliance with the RTA Protocol is not possible before the expiry of a limitation period and proceedings are started in accordance with paragraph 16 of this Practice Direction.

1.2

A claim under this Practice Direction must be started in a county court and will normally be heard by a district judge.

Modification of Part 8

2.1

The claim is made under the Part 8 procedure as modified by this Practice Direction and subject to paragraph 2.2.

2.2

The claim will be determined by the court on the contents of the Court Proceedings Pack. The following rules do not apply to a claim under this Practice Direction –

(1)   rule 8.2A (issue of claim form without naming defendants);

(2)   rule 8.3 (acknowledgment of service);

(3)   rule 8.5 (filing and serving written evidence);

(4)   rule 8.6 (evidence – general);

(5)   rule 8.7 (part 20 claims);

(6)   rule 8.8 (procedure where defendant objects to use of the Part 8 procedure); and

(7)   rule 8.9(c).

Definitions

3.1

References to 'the Court Proceedings Pack (Part A) Form', 'the Court Proceedings Pack (Part B) Form' and 'the CNF Response Form' are references to the forms used in the RTA Protocol.

3.2

'RTA Protocol offer' has the meaning given by rule 36.17.

3.3

'Settlement hearing' means a hearing where the court considers a settlement agreed between the parties (whether before or after proceedings have started) and the claimant is a child.

3.4

'Stage 3 hearing' means a final hearing to determine the amount of damages that remain in dispute between the parties.

Types of claim in which this modified Part 8 procedure may be followed

4.1

The court may at any stage order a claim that has been started under Part 7 to continue under the Part 8 procedure as modified by this Practice Direction.

An application to the court to determine the amount of damages

5.1

An application to the court to determine the amount of damages must be started by a claim form.

5.2

The claim form must state –

(1)   that the claimant has followed the procedure set out in the RTA Protocol;

(2)   the date when the Court Proceedings Pack (Part A and Part B) Form

was sent to the defendant. (This provision does not apply where the claimant is a child and the application is for a settlement hearing);

(3)   whether the claimant wants the claim to be determined by the court on the papers (except where a party is a child) or at a Stage 3 hearing;

(4)   where the claimant seeks a settlement hearing or a Stage 3 hearing, the dates which the claimant requests should be avoided; and

(5)   the value of the claim.

Filing and serving written evidence

6.1

The claimant must file with the claim form –

(1)   the Court Proceedings Pack (Part A) Form;

(2)   the Court Proceedings Pack (Part B) Form (the claimant and defendant's final offers) in a sealed envelope. (This provision does not apply where the claimant is a child and the application is for a settlement hearing);

(3)   copies of medical reports;

(4)   evidence of special damages;

(5)   evidence of disbursements (for example the cost of any medical report) in accordance with rule 45.30(2); and

(6)   any notice of funding.

6.2

The filing of the claim form and documents set out in paragraph 6.1 represent the start of Stage 3 for the purposes of fixed costs.

6.3

Subject to paragraph 6.5 the claimant must only file those documents in paragraph 6.1 where they have already been sent to the defendant under the RTA Protocol.

6.4

The claimant's evidence as set out in paragraph 6.1 must be served on the defendant with the claim form.

6.5

Where the claimant is a child the claimant must also provide to the court the following in relation to a settlement made before or after the start of proceedings –

(1)   the draft consent order;

(2)   the advice by counsel, solicitor or other legal representative on the amount of damages; and

(3)   a statement verified by a statement of truth signed by the litigation friend which confirms whether the child has recovered in accordance with the prognosis and whether there are any continuing symptoms. This statement will enable the court to decide whether to order the child to attend the settlement hearing.

6.6

Where the defendant is uninsured and the Motor Insurers' Bureau ('MIB') or its agents have consented in the CNF Response Form to the MIB being joined as a defendant, the claimant must name the MIB as the second defendant and must also provide to the court a copy of the CNF Response Form completed by or on behalf of the MIB.

6.7

Where this Practice Direction requires a step to be taken by the defendant, it will be sufficient for this step to be taken by the MIB.

Evidence – general

7.1

The parties may not rely upon evidence unless –

(1)   it has been served in accordance with paragraph 6.4;

(2)   it has been filed in accordance with paragraph 8.2 and 11.3; or

(3)   (where the court considers that it cannot properly determine the claim without it), the court orders otherwise and gives directions.

7.2

Where the court considers that –

(1)   further evidence must be provided by any party; and

(2)   the claim is not suitable to continue under the Stage 3 Procedure,

the court will order that the claim will continue under Part 7, allocate the claim to a track and give directions.

7.3

Where paragraph 7.2 applies the court will not allow the Stage 3 fixed costs.

Acknowledgment of Service

8.1

The defendant must file and serve an acknowledgment of service in Form N210B not more than 14 days after service of the claim form.

8.2

The defendant must file and serve –

(1)   with the acknowledgment of service, any notice of funding; and

(2)   with the acknowledgment of service, or as soon as possible thereafter, a certificate that is in force.

('Certificate' is defined in rule 36.15(1)(e)(i).)

8.3

The acknowledgment of service must state whether the defendant –

(1)

      (a)   contests the amount of damages claimed;

      (b)   contests the making of an order for damages;

      (c)   disputes the court's jurisdiction; or

      (d)   objects to the use of the Stage 3 Procedure;

(2)   wants the claim to be determined by the court on the papers or at a Stage 3 hearing.

8.4

Where the defendant objects to the use of the Stage 3 Procedure reasons must be given in the acknowledgment of service.

8.5

The acknowledgment of service may be signed and filed by the defendant's insurer who may give their address as the address for service.

Dismissal of the claim

9.1

Where the defendant opposes the claim because the claimant has –

(1)   not followed the procedure set out in the RTA Protocol; or

(2)   filed and served additional or new evidence with the claim form that had not been provided under the RTA Protocol,

the court will dismiss the claim and the claimant may start proceedings under Part 7.

(Rule 45.36 sets out the costs consequences of failing to comply with the RTA Protocol.)

Withdrawal of the RTA Protocol offer

10.1

A party may only withdraw an RTA Protocol offer after proceedings have started with the court's permission. Where the court gives permission the claim will no longer continue under the Stage 3 Procedure and the court will give directions. The court will only give permission where there is good reason for the claim not to continue under the Stage 3 Procedure.

Consideration of the claim

11.1

The court will order that damages are to be assessed –

(1)   on the papers; or

(2)   at a Stage 3 hearing where –

    (a)   the claimant so requests on the claim form;

    (b)   the defendant so requests in the acknowledgment of service (Form N210B); or

    (c)   the court so orders,

and on a date determined by the court.

11.2

The court will give the parties at least 21 days notice of the date of the determination on the papers or the date of the Stage 3 hearing.

11.3

Where further deductible amounts have accrued since the final offer was made by both parties in the Court Proceedings Pack (Part B) Form, the defendant must file an up to date certificate at least 5 days before the date of a determination on the papers.

11.4

Where the claim is determined on the papers the court will give reasons for its decision in the judgment.

('Deductible amount' is defined in rule 36.15(1)(d).)

Settlement at Stage 2 where the claimant is a child

12.1

Paragraphs 12.2 to 12.5 apply where –

(1)   the claimant is a child;

(2)   there is a settlement at Stage 2 of the RTA Protocol; and

(3)   an application is made to the court to approve the settlement.

12.2

Where the settlement is approved at the settlement hearing the court will order the costs to be paid in accordance with rule 45.33(2).

12.3

Where the settlement is not approved at the first settlement hearing and the court orders a second settlement hearing at which the settlement is approved, the court will order the costs to be paid in accordance with rule 45.33(4) to (6).

12.4

Where the settlement is not approved at the first settlement hearing and the court orders that the claim is not suitable to be determined under the Stage 3 Procedure, the court will order costs to be paid in accordance with rule 45.35 and will give directions.

12.5

Where the settlement is not approved at the second settlement hearing the claim will no longer continue under the Stage 3 Procedure and the court will give directions.

Settlement at Stage 3 where the claimant is a child

13.1

Paragraphs 13.2 and 13.3 apply where –

(1)   the claimant is a child;

(2)   there is a settlement after proceedings have started under the Stage 3 Procedure; and

(3)   an application is made to the court to approve the settlement.

13.2

Where the settlement is approved at the settlement hearing the court will order the costs to be paid in accordance with rule 45.34(2).

13.3

Where the settlement is not approved at the settlement hearing the court will order the claim to proceed to a Stage 3 hearing.

Adjournment

14.1

Where the court adjourns a settlement hearing or a Stage 3 hearing it may, in its discretion, order the costs to be paid in accordance with rule 45.39.

Appeals – determination on the papers

15.1

The court will not consider an application to set aside a judgment made after a determination on the papers. The judgment will state the appeal court to which an appeal lies.

Limitation

16.1

Where compliance with the RTA Protocol is not possible before the expiry of a limitation period the claimant may start proceedings in accordance with paragraph 16.2.

16.2

The claimant must –

(1)   start proceedings under this Practice Direction; and

(2)   state on the claim form that –

   (a)   the claim is for damages; and

   (b)   a stay of proceedings is sought in order to comply with the RTA Protocol.

16.3

The claimant must send to the defendant the claim form together with the order imposing the stay.

16.4

Where a claim is made under paragraph 16.1 the provisions in this Practice Direction, except paragraphs 1.2, 2.1, 2.2 and 16.1 to 16.6, are disapplied.

16.5

Where –

(1)   a stay is granted by the court;

(2)   the parties have complied with the RTA Protocol; and

(3)   the claimant wishes to start the Stage 3 Procedure,

the claimant must make an application to the court to lift the stay and request directions.

16.6

Where the court orders that the stay be lifted –

(1)   the provisions of this Practice Direction will apply; and

(2)   the claimant must –

    (a)   amend the claim form in accordance with paragraph 5.2; and

    (b)   file the documents in paragraph 6.1.

16.7

Where, during Stage 1 or Stage 2 of the RTA Protocol –

(1)   the claim no longer continues under that Protocol; and

(2)   the claimant wishes to start proceedings under Part 7,

the claimant must make an application to the court to lift the stay and request directions.

Modification to the general rules

17.1

The claim will not be allocated to a track. Parts 26 to 29 do not apply.

7 Investigating the Claim and the Pre-Action Protocol for Personal Injury Claims

This chapter considers the basic practical steps which will be needed in every personal injury action, up to the stage of deciding to take court proceedings. Some cases will, of course, never go further than this. Road traffic accident claims of a value of less than £10,000 are dealt with under the procedure described in Chapter 6.

7.1 Taking instructions

The following vital matters should be attended to at the first meeting with the client.

7.1.1 Conflicts of interest and confirming the client's identity

Check that neither you nor a colleague has been instructed by anyone with an actual or probable conflicting interest in the matter. Otherwise, you may disqualify your firm from acting for either party. Further, you are under a duty to confirm the client's identity by asking for proof.

7.1.2 Financing the case

The client must be informed as soon as possible how the claim is to be financed and of his or her potential liability to costs. Advise the client carefully. Some conditional fee insurers insist that the conditional fee agreement and the insurance policy are taken out before any steps are taken to investigate the claim. The policy that you intend to use must be checked. Further, the client must be advised as to liability for both his or her own and the opponent's costs. See, generally, Chapter 5.

7.1.3 Taking instructions

Many firms now use a standard questionnaire to ensure that important issues are not overlooked (see para 7.9). At an early stage, it is prudent to obtain the client's statement.

Allow the client to tell the basic story in his or her own words at the first meeting. However, once the client is at ease and the basic history is understood, full details are needed of:

(a) pre-accident work, state of health and lifestyle;

(b) what the client remembers of the accident, details of any witnesses and whether the accident was reported to the police or Health and Safety Executive;

(c) details of the injuries and treatment;

(d) the consequences in terms of time off work, expenses and benefits received, and effect on the client's leisure activities.

Do not worry if some information would be inadmissible in court, but it should be ensured that the client reads the statement and signs and dates it. This will protect you if the client later changes the story; further, if the client dies or becomes unable to give evidence before the trial, the statement can still be admissible as evidence under the Civil Evidence Acts 1968 and 1995.

7.1.4 Initial advice

It should be possible in many cases to give the client some idea of the chances of success on liability at the first interview or soon afterwards. It is generally wise, however, to defer any definite advice on the value of the claim until a medical report and information on special damages has been obtained.

7.2 Preliminary correspondence

7.2.1 Contacting witnesses

Witnesses should be interviewed, and signed and dated statements taken from them for the reasons set out above. There is nothing to stop you interviewing someone who has already given a statement to another party: there is no property in a witness. Although other employees, for instance, may be reluctant to give evidence against the employer, they should be reminded that they can, if necessary, be compelled to attend court to give evidence.

7.2.2 Obtaining reports

If the accident happened on a public road, it should have been reported to the police. The police report will normally be available from the chief constable once any criminal proceedings are completed or the police have decided not to prosecute. The report will contain details of the vehicles, the parties and their insurers, the accident scene, a plan and sometimes photographs of the scene, the views of the investigating officer as to the cause of the accident and, often, statements by those involved and any witnesses. If the case becomes defended, it is possible to take further statements from the investigating officer on payment of a further fee and submitting the statement to the police for checking.

In the case of industrial accidents, ask to see the employer's accident book and, in the case of major incidents, ask the Health and Safety Executive whether the notification form (Form 2058) has been submitted, and whether it can release any statements or photographs.

It may also be advisable to instruct expert witnesses at this stage.

7.2.3 Details of special damages

It will be necessary to write to the claimant's employers for details of pre- and post-accident earnings and of any statutory sick pay received; to the CRU for details of state benefits (for the address, see Appendix 1); and to the claimant's tax office for confirmation of any tax rebates paid.

7.2.4 Letter before action

Once the claimant's solicitor is satisfied that the claimant has a cause of action, the solicitor should write formally to the defendant (or the defendant's solicitor or insurer). There are special procedures that have to be followed when the claim is a road traffic claim. Where a claimant is on a conditional fee basis, this must be notified to the defendants in the preliminary letter.

7.3 Terms of Pre-Action Protocol for Personal Injury Claims (Pre-Action Protocol)

7.3.1 Aims of Pre-Action Protocol

The Pre-Action Protocol for Personal Injury Claims applies to all claims where the claimant has suffered a personal injury (see para 7.12). However, it should be noted that the Pre-Action Protocol for Low Value Personal Injury Claims in Road Traffic Accidents should be used where there has been a road traffic accident and the value of the claim is less than £10,000 (see Chapter 6). The aims of the Pre-Action Protocol are:

(a)   to encourage more contact between the parties before the issue of proceedings;

(b)   a better and earlier exchange of information;

(c)   better pre-action investigation by both sides;

(d)   to put the parties in a position where they may be able to settle cases fairly and early without litigation; and

(e)   to enable proceedings to run to the court's timetable and efficiently, if litigation does become necessary.

The Pre-Action Protocol applies to all fast track personal injury claims (except those governed by the road traffic procedure, see Chapter 6), and the spirit of the Protocol is expected to be followed for multi track claims. Where a practitioner does not use the Pre-Action Protocol, a reason must be given and the court will look at the effect of non-compliance on the other party when deciding whether to impose cost sanctions.

7.3.2   Letter of claim

As soon as sufficient information is available, the letter of claim should be prepared, in which enough information should be given to allow the insurers broadly to value their risk. The Pre-Action Protocol recommends a standard format be used. Two copies of the letter of claim should be sent to the defendant, one being intended for the defendant's insurers. Best practice will be to identify the insurers as quickly as possible and write to them direct, as well as the defendant.

The letter of claim should:

(a)   ask for insurance details;

(b)   request that the accompanying letter be forwarded to the insurers;

(c)   contain a clear summary of the facts on which the claim is based;

(d)   indicate the nature of any injuries suffered and of any financial loss incurred.

After acknowledging the claim, the defendant has 3 months to investigate the matter and comment on whether or not liability is accepted. The letter of claim does not have any status as a pleading; however, any discrepancies will provide ammunition for cross-examination and the costs application, so accuracy is of paramount importance.

The defendant must respond to the letter of claim within 21 days identifying the insurer. If no reply is received, the claim may proceed without risk of costs penalisation.

7.3.3 Disclosure

The letter of claim includes a provision for disclosure of standard documents relevant to the type of incident complained of. If the defendant denies liability, copies of these documents and copies of others in his or her possession which are clearly relevant to the issues between the parties should be enclosed with the letter of reply. The documents to be disclosed are those which will be likely to be ordered as disclosed by the court, either on an application for pre-action disclosure or on disclosure during the proceedings.

7.3.4 Financial losses

The Pre-Action Protocol provides that a schedule of supplementary documents should be submitted as soon as possible:

(a) outline details of special damages should be given in the letter of claim;

(b) a full schedule should be provided if the defendant admits liability or an early interim payment is requested;

(c) if the case is capable of settlement before proceedings because the claimant's prognosis is certain, it is best to provide a full schedule together with medical evidence and a Part 36 offer to settle the claim before proceedings are issued.

7.3.5 Expert evidence

The Pre-Action Protocol envisages the use of expert evidence with the choice of expert being agreed between the parties.

The claimant's lawyer should:

(a) seek medical records;

(b) identify at least one, and preferably two alternative experts in the same specialty;

(c) write to the defendant giving the names of the proposed experts.

The defendant has 14 days to accept, reject or suggest other named experts. If the defendant does not reply or objects to all the experts, then the parties may instruct experts of their own choice and the court will decide, if proceedings are issued, whether either party has acted unreasonably. If the defendant does not object to the expert, he or she will not be entitled to rely on his or her own expert evidence unless the claimant agrees, the court directs or the first party is not prepared to disclose the original report.

Written questions

Where an agreed expert is instructed, either party may send to the expert written questions on the report, relevant to the issues, via the first party's solicitors. The expert should send answers to the questions separately and directly to each party

7.4 Other preliminary steps

7.4.1 Inspecting the accident scene

It is useful for the lawyers involved to have familiarised themselves with the accident site and for photographs and a plan to be drawn up as soon as possible after the accident to capture important features such as tyre skid marks on the road. These should be agreed, if possible, in order that they may be used in evidence at any trial without difficulty.

In accidents-at-work cases, the inspection may be in the company of the expert(s) instructed by one or both parties; however, it is becoming increasingly difficult to obtain leave to adduce expert evidence at trial and it may be that the lawyers attend with a camera. In any case, it is important to ensure that the inspection keeps to the fact-finding role and does not broaden out into an informal 'arbitration' as to who was to blame.

In factory cases, too, the defendant or the defendant's insurers may be reluctant to allow an inspection. In this case, the claimant's solicitors should threaten and, if necessary, apply to the court under section 52 of the County Courts Act 1984 for an order for inspecting, photographing, preserving, sampling or experimenting with any property which may be relevant in later proceedings, for example, the machine alleged to have caused the injuries.

7.4.2 Pre-action disclosure

Again, in accidents-at-work cases, the defendant may have documents, such as safety committee minutes, relating to both the present and perhaps previous similar accidents that may indicate, for example, an unsafe system of work. The defendant may refuse to disclose whether there are such documents until the normal discovery stage after the case has begun.

The claimant may obtain this evidence by pre-action discovery:

(a) the defendant must first be asked to provide the documents voluntarily, usually in the letter of claim;

(b) if the documents are not forthcoming within a reasonable time, an originating summons should be taken out and served with a supporting affidavit.

The court will order production of the documents only where it is satisfied that:

(a) the defendant possesses the documents or they are in his or her custody or control;

(b) disclosure of the documents is necessary prior to proceedings being issued;

(c) the two parties are likely to become parties in the action. The statement supporting the application should:

    (i) explain in some detail the reasons for anticipating that there is likely to be a claim;

    (ii) explain why the documentation is necessary to assist in making a claim;

    (iii) explain the need for urgency, if such is the case;

    (iv) explain why it is believed that the defendant has the documents in his or her power, possession or control.

7.4.3   Attending other proceedings

It is important to ascertain the outcome of any criminal proceedings (such as careless driving or breaches of health and safety regulations) against one or both of the parties, since relevant convictions may be admissible in the civil proceedings. Further, attendance at such proceedings, and at proceedings such as inquests which have no formal effect on civil proceedings, may give an early idea of the available evidence.

7.5   Instructing expert witnesses

7.5.1   Preliminary matters

An expert medical report will be needed in all personal injury cases. A report from a consulting engineer may be needed in some work-accident claims and, very rarely, in some road-accident cases. The parties should always be aware that the court will be anxious to limit the use of expert evidence and consider whether it is possible to agree on the use of a joint expert. See, also, the obligations to inform the defendant and agree the choice of expert (para 7.3.5).

It is wise to check with the expert on the likely amount of the fee. The client's express authority to instruct the expert should be obtained, and in both private and legal aid cases, the client should be warned, where appropriate, that the cost may not be recoverable from the defendant.

7.5.2 Instructing doctors

In all but the most trivial cases, a report from a consultant rather than the claimant's general practitioner will be needed. In most cases, where limbs have been broken, the basic report should be from an orthopaedic surgeon. More specialised reports may also be needed, for example, from a neuro-surgeon and, possibly, a clinical psychologist where brain damage is suspected, or from a psychiatrist where personality change is alleged.

Care should be taken to instruct a consultant who understands the demands of a forensic medical report, and understands the duties that an expert owes to the court.

When instructing the doctor, there is a model letter set out in the Pre-Action Protocol. The basic history of the accident should be described and the client's statement should be enclosed, in the case of the claimant informing the doctor of the claimant's pre- and post-accident lifestyle. Also, the doctor should be asked to consider whether the case would be suitable for an award of provisional damages if there is any real risk that the claimant's condition may seriously worsen later. Finally, the claimant's consent for the hospital to disclose his or her records should be enclosed.

On receiving the report, it should be gone through carefully with the client, unless the doctor has said that any parts of it are not to be communicated to the client.

The following terms are commonly found in reports (for more detail see, for example, the *Longman Medical Dictionary* (Clio Press, ISIS Large Print Books, 1988) and the diagrams in Kemp & Kemp, *The Quantum of Damages* (looseleaf, Sweet & Maxwell) or *Butterworths Personal Injury Litigation Service* (looseleaf, LexisNexis, Butterworths)):

- abduction: moving a limb away from the *medial* line;

- adduction: moving a limb towards the medial line;

- ataxia: loss of control of movement due to sensory defects;

- avulsion: a tearing;

- callus: bony material between ends of a fractured bone when healing;

- cicatrix: scar;

- Colles' fracture: fracture of wrist across the lower end of the radius;

- comminuted: bone fractured into several pieces;

- crepitus: grating of bone against bone or roughened cartilage;

- dorsiflexion: backward movement;

- embolism: blockage of small blood vessels;

- excise: to cut surgically;

- extension: straightening of a joint;

- fibrosis: thickening of tissue;

- flexion: bending of a joint;

- gluteal: of the buttock;

- ilium: hip bone;

- labial: of the lips;

- lesion: change in functions or texture of organs;

- lumbar: of the loins;

- manipulation: movement of a joint to reduce stiffness;

- node: small knot of tissue;

- odema: swelling due to build-up of fluid;

- parietal: referable to the inner walls of a body cavity;

- plantar: of sole of foot;

- pleural cavity: space between lungs and inner chest wall;

- pulmonary: of the lung;

- reduction: bringing back to normal position;

- sacrum: five fused vertebrae at base of spine;

- spondylosis: arthritis of the spine;

- thorax: of the chest;

- ulna: inner bone of the forearm;

- ureter: tubes taking urine from the pelvis to the bladder.

It should be checked that the doctor has not discussed the cause of the accident, that there is no substantial disagreement between the doctor's and the claimant's account of the claimant's present condition and any suggestion by the doctor that the claimant is exaggerating the symptoms.

The doctor should be contacted if there are such disagreements, or points in the report that are not clear (although be aware that this correspondence may be disclosed to the court). It is permissible to raise questions of a doctor instructed by the other side.

Where the defendant wishes to instruct a doctor to examine the claimant

The defendant's advisers may want a report from a doctor instructed by them. Although they cannot insist on this and will have to persuade the court that such a report is needed, they can seek a stay of the action until the claimant undergoes a medical examination, unless the claimant's objection is a reasonable objection to being examined by a particular doctor, for example, on the ground of a real risk of bias against the claimant.

However, the claimant can insist on the following conditions:

(a)   the claimant's expenses and any loss of earnings are paid;

(b)   no one apart from the defendant's doctor is present;

(c)   if the claimant is a minor, his or her parent can also be present;

(d)   the doctor will not discuss the causes of the accident.

7.5.3   Instructing engineers

It should be considered carefully whether an expert's report is necessary. The use of the expert must be justified to the court and the court may not admit the evidence or, alternatively, costs may not be recovered. It is essential to instruct an expert in the appropriate field (for example, mechanical or mining engineering) and who has experience of preparing reports for litigation.

Also, the engineer must be given as much information about the case as possible, although it must be remembered that the letter of instruction may have to be disclosed to the court.

An inspection of the site should be arranged, and the defendant's undertaking should be obtained that the relevant features such as the machine allegedly involved should not be altered in the meantime. It should be ensured that the expert is made clear as to the issues on which advice is required. The report should be checked when received and it should be ensured that the client understands its implications.

7.6   Negotiations

7.6.1   'Without prejudice' correspondence

Most of these claims, if successful, will ultimately be paid by insurers and will be handled initially by insurance companies' claims departments. It is their usual practice to conduct correspondence, often right up to settlement of the case, on the basis of a denial of liability and under the heading 'without prejudice'.

The effect of without prejudice correspondence is that the production of letters during proceedings is not permitted, except when proving the making of and the terms of any settlement reached (*Rush & Winipkins v GLC* [1987] 2 WLR 533, CA). The privilege is attracted by any letter or other communication intended to make concessions or other attempts at reaching a settlement of the claim. However, it is prudent to expressly use the words 'without prejudice'.

7.6.2   Tactics

Advisers of the claimant in personal injury cases should always aim to keep up the pressure on their opponent if the defendant fails to comply with the Pre-Action Protocol, to reply to correspondence or to deny liability. In order to do this, it is more effective for the claimant to serve proceedings promptly, rather than to engage in protracted correspondence.

One, very real, problem is that insurance companies will claim that departments are often overworked and do not reply to correspondence. The only way of progressing the matter is to issue proceedings.

7.6.3   Discussion 'without prejudice'

Insurers or their solicitors will frequently seek to dispose of cases by making a Part 36 offer (see Chapter 10) or by telephoning and discussing possible terms of settlement. It is important that both sides prepare thoroughly for such a meeting, checking the relevant law, the various heads of damage claimed and the current level of interest that would be awarded and of costs incurred. The defendant's representatives are likely to be well informed as to the going figure for the type of injuries in question, but there is likely to be scope for argument over the amount of contributory negligence, if any, and of the more speculative heads of damage. The claimant's lawyer should allow the defendant's lawyer to make the first offer. This is unlikely to be the last one, and it may be increased slightly if the claimant is advised not to accept it.

Once a definite offer has been made, the claimant's adviser should seek the client's instructions on it, explaining in particular the impact, if any, of the legal aid charge in respect of any costs not recovered from the defendant. Counsel's advice on the reasonableness of the settlement should be taken in more complex cases. The solicitor's oral advice should be confirmed in writing. If the client rejects the offer against this advice, he or she should be warned of the consequences, such as the risk of losing at trial and therefore receiving nothing, as well as the costs penalties (see para 10.1.6).

Settlement meeting

Many major claims now settle by way of a 'round table meeting' where the parties and their legal representatives meet and discuss settlement. Sometimes this is done with a mediator present. It is important that the parties prepare properly for such hearings.

7.7   Instructing counsel

7.7.1   When to use counsel

Counsel are frequently instructed to advise on liability and quantum of damages at the outset of a personal injury action. Such advice is usually in writing, a conference being reserved until a trial is in prospect. However, in difficult cases where the success of the party's case may depend, for example, on the party's credibility as a witness, it is helpful to have a conference and, perhaps, advice on evidence, at an earlier stage. Counsel will therefore be aware of the case when asked to draft the pleadings, and the client will be more confident that the case is being handled by someone who is familiar with it and whom he or she has met before the trial.

An added advantage for the solicitor is that, if the case goes wrong through the action of counsel, the solicitor should be immune from liability in negligence, provided competent counsel was instructed and competently briefed (*Re A (A Minor)* (1988) NLJ, 18 March, CA). The choice of counsel is very important and care should be taken to ensure that someone who practises predominantly in personal injury litigation is instructed. Particular care should be taken to instruct more specialist counsel in complex employer's liability, high value or medical negligence cases.

7.7.2   How to instruct counsel

Instructions should enclose all the relevant documents including the statements of the client and any witnesses, the police or Health and Safety Executive's and engineer's reports, the medical report(s), a calculation of special damage, any legal aid certificate and relevant correspondence with the other side. If the matter is funded on a conditional fee basis, a copy of the conditional fee agreement should be enclosed. Instructions should not merely be a back sheet enclosing all the papers, but be self-contained and self-explanatory, outlining the facts and the available evidence and specifying what counsel is being asked to do. This will minimise the difficulties if another counsel has to take over the case at a later date.

Once received, counsel's advice should be discussed with the client and its implications explained.

7.8   Decision to issue proceedings

7.8.1   To sue or not to sue?

The decision must obviously be the client's, but should be made with the benefit of the solicitor's and, where necessary, counsel's advice, both oral and written. In particular, the risks of costs must be considered in both private and legally aided cases, since legal aid contributions are now payable for the duration of a case. On the other hand, it may be essential to start proceedings because the limitation period is about to expire, or it may be desirable to do so to put pressure on the defendant to settle.

7.8.2   Where to issue proceedings

Both the High Court and county courts now have unlimited jurisdiction in personal injury actions; however, all personal injury actions for less than £50,000 must be issued in county courts. In deciding the value of the action for the purpose of issuing proceedings:

(a)   no account is taken of any possible finding of contributory negligence – except if contributory negligence is admitted;

(b)   where the claimant seeks provisional damages, no account is taken of the possibility of a future application for further damages;

(c)   interest and costs are disregarded;

(d)   sums liable to recoupment are taken into account.

If the claimant issues in the High Court when the action does not exceed £50,000, he or she risks having his or her costs reduced on any taxation of the action or having the case struck out.

There are no longer any geographical restrictions on the issue of an action and proceedings can be issued in any county court. However, the action can be transferred to another county court for reasons of convenience or if the court thinks it best to be in a court near the accident scene.

7.9   Client questionnaire checklist

General information

- Full name.
- Proof of identity.
- Litigation friend's full name (if appropriate, ie if the claimant is a child or has a mental disability).
- Address of client (and/or litigation friend).
- Telephone number and email address (if appropriate).
- Date of birth.
- National Insurance number.
- Marital status.
- Date and time of accident.
- Place of accident.
- Employer's name and address.
- Occupation.
- Accountant's name and address (self-employed claimant).
- Is client registered for VAT?
- Funding – is client a member of a motoring organisation/legal expenses insurance company? Is there any insurance available from other sources, for example, home policy or motor policy?
- Funding – is client eligible for Community Legal Service (see para 5.3)?
- Funding – private/payment on account/payment for disbursements.
- Funding – is a conditional fee agreement appropriate?
- Circumstances of accident.
- Names and addresses of any witnesses.

7.10 Letter of claim checklist

The letter of claim should contain:

- A clear summary of the facts on which the claim is based.

- An indication of the nature of any injuries suffered and financial loss incurred.

- Details of client's employment, loss of earnings and any other losses.

- An offer to provide a copy of a police report, if obtained, if the defendant pays half the fee for obtaining it.

- A list of documents the defendant is expected to disclose.

- Details of the insurer should be asked for.

Also:

- The defendant must be told that the letter begins a timetable and that acknowledgement of receipt of letter must be within 21 days.

- The letter must be sent in duplicate and the defendant requested to send a copy to his or her insurers. If the insurers are known at the outset, a copy should be sent to them directly.

7.11 Key points

- Both parties must strive to ensure that they comply with both the letter and the spirit of the Pre-Action Protocol.

- The letter of claim must contain sufficient information to enable the defendant to determine the facts and assess the risk.

- There is a standard procedure for choosing medical experts (see para 7.5).

- Without prejudice negotiations often lead to the early settlement of cases.

7.12 Civil Procedure Rules Pre-Action Protocol for Personal Injury Claims

Contents

1 INTRODUCTION

1.1

Lord Woolf in his final Access to Justice Report of July 1996 recommended the development of pre-action protocols:

To build on and increase the benefits of early but well informed settlement which genuinely satisfy both parties to dispute.

1.2

The aims of pre-action protocols are:

- more pre-action contact between the parties
- better and earlier exchange of information
- better pre-action investigation by both sides
- to put the parties in a position where they may be able to settle cases fairly and early without litigation
- to enable proceedings to run to the court's timetable and efficiently, if litigation does become necessary

- to promote the provision of medical or rehabilitation treatment (not just in high value cases) to address the needs of the claimant

1.3

The concept of protocols is relevant to a range of initiatives for good litigation and pre-litigation practice, especially:

- predictability in the time needed for steps pre-proceedings
- standardisation of relevant information, including documents to be disclosed.

1.4

The Courts will be able to treat the standards set in protocols as the normal reasonable approach to pre-action conduct. If proceedings are issued, it will be for the court to decide whether non-compliance with a protocol should merit adverse consequences. Guidance on the court's likely approach will be given from time to time in practice directions.

1.5

If the court has to consider the question of compliance after proceedings have begun, it will not be concerned with minor infringements, e.g. failure by a short period to provide relevant information. One minor breach will not exempt the 'innocent' party from following the protocol. The court will look at the effect of non-compliance on the other party when deciding whether to impose sanctions.

2 NOTES OF GUIDANCE

2.1

The protocol has been kept deliberately simple to promote ease of use and general acceptability. The notes of guidance which follows relate particularly to issues which arose during the piloting of the protocol.

Scope of the Protocol

2.2

This protocol is intended to apply to all claims which include a claim for personal injury (except those claims covered by the Clinical Disputes and Disease and Illness Protocols) and to the entirety of those claims: not only to the personal injury element of a claim which also includes, for instance, property damage.

2.3

This protocol is primarily designed for those road traffic, tripping and slipping and accident at work cases which include an element of personal injury with a value of less than the fast track limit and which are likely to be allocated to that track. This is because time will be of the essence, after proceedings are issued, especially for the defendant, if a case is to be ready for trial within 30 weeks of allocation. Also, proportionality of work and costs to the value of what is in dispute is particularly important in lower value claims. For some claims within the value 'scope' of the fast track some flexibility in the timescale of the protocol may be necessary, see also paragraph 3.8.

2.4

However, the 'cards on the table' approach advocated by the protocol is equally appropriate to higher value claims. The spirit, if not the letter of the protocol, should still be followed for multi-track type claims. In accordance with the sense of the civil justice reforms, the court will expect to see the spirit of reasonable pre-action behaviour applied in all cases, regardless of the existence of a specific protocol. In particular with regard to personal injury cases with a value of more than the fast track limit, to avoid the necessity of proceedings parties are expected to comply with the protocol as far as possible e.g. in respect of letters before action, exchanging information and documents and agreeing experts.

2.5

The timetable and the arrangements for disclosing documents and obtaining expert evidence may need to be varied to suit the circumstances of the case. Where one or both parties consider the detail of the protocol is not appropriate to the case, and proceedings are subsequently issued, the court will expect an explanation as to why the protocol has not been followed, or has been varied.

Early Notification

2.6

The claimant's legal representative may wish to notify the defendant and/or his insurer as soon as they know a claim is likely to be made, but before they are able to send a detailed letter of claim, particularly for instance, when the defendant has no or limited knowledge of the incident giving rise to the claim or where the claimant is incurring significant expenditure as a result of the accident which he hopes the defendant might pay for, in whole or in part. If the claimant's representative chooses to do this, it will not start the timetable for responding.

The Letter of Claim

2.7

The specimen letter of claim at Annex A will usually be sent to the individual defendant. In practice, he/she may have no personal financial interest in the financial outcome of the claim/dispute because he/she is insured. Court imposed sanctions for non-compliance with the protocol may be ineffective against an insured. This is why the protocol emphasises the importance of passing the letter of claim to the insurer and the possibility that the insurance cover might be affected. If an insurer receives the letter of claim only after some delay by the insured, it would not be unreasonable for the insurer to ask the claimant for additional time to respond.

2.8

In road traffic cases, the letter of claim should always contain the name and address of the hospital where the claimant was treated and, where available, the claimant's hospital reference number.

2.9

The priority at letter of claim stage is for the claimant to provide sufficient information for the defendant to assess liability. Sufficient information should also be provided to enable the defendant to estimate the likely size of the claim.

2.10

Once the claimant has sent the letter of claim no further investigation on liability should normally be carried out until a response is received from the defendant indicating whether liability is disputed.

2.10A

Where a claim no longer continues under the Pre-Action Protocol for Low Value Personal Injury Claims in Road Traffic Accidents the Claim Notification Form ('CNF') completed by the claimant under that Protocol can be used as the letter of claim under this Protocol unless the defendant has notified the claimant that there is inadequate information in the CNF.

Reasons for Early Issue

2.11

The protocol recommends that a defendant be given three months to investigate and respond to a claim before proceedings are issued. This may not always be possible, particularly where a claimant only consults a solicitor close to the end of any relevant limitation period. In these circumstances, the claimant's solicitor should give as much notice of the intention to issue proceedings as is practicable and the parties should consider whether the court might be invited to extend time for service of the claimant's supporting documents and for service of any defence, or alternatively, to stay the proceedings while the recommended steps in the protocol are followed.

Status of Letters of Claim and Response

2.12

Letters of claim and response are not intended to have the same status as a statement of case in proceedings. Matters may come to light as a result of investigation after the letter of claim has been sent, or after the defendant has responded, particularly if disclosure of documents takes place outside the recommended three-month period. These circumstances could mean that the 'pleaded' case of one or both parties is presented slightly differently than in the letter of claim and response. It would not be consistent with the spirit of the protocol for a party to 'take a point' on this in the proceedings, provided that there was no obvious intention by the party who changed their position to mislead the other party.

Disclosure of Documents

2.13

The aim of the early disclosure of documents by the defendant is not to encourage 'fishing expeditions' by the claimant, but to promote an early exchange of relevant information to help in clarifying or resolving issues in dispute. The claimant's solicitor can assist by identifying in the letter of claim or in a subsequent letter the particular categories of documents which they consider are relevant.

Experts

2.14

The protocol encourages joint selection of, and access to, experts. The report produced is not a joint report for the purposes of CPR Part 35. Most frequently this will apply to the medical expert, but on occasions also to liability experts, e.g. engineers. The protocol promotes the practice of the claimant obtaining a medical report, disclosing it to the defendant who then asks questions and/or agrees it and does not obtain his own report. The Protocol provides for nomination of the expert by the claimant in personal injury claims because of the early stage of the proceedings and the particular nature of such claims. If proceedings have to be issued, a medical report must be attached to these proceedings. However, if necessary after proceedings have commenced and with the permission of the court, the parties may obtain further expert reports. It would be for the court to decide whether the costs of more than one expert's report should be recoverable.

2.15

Some solicitors choose to obtain medical reports through medical agencies, rather than directly from a specific doctor or hospital. The defendant's prior consent to the action should be sought and, if the defendant so requests, the agency should be asked to provide in advance the names of the doctor(s) whom they are considering instructing.

Alternative Dispute Resolution

2.16

The parties should consider whether some form of alternative dispute resolution procedure would be more suitable than litigation, and if so, endeavour to agree which form to adopt. Both the Claimant and Defendant may be required by the Court to provide evidence that alternative means of resolving their dispute were considered. The Courts take the view that litigation should be a last resort, and that claims should not be issued prematurely when a settlement is still actively being explored. Parties are warned that if the protocol is not followed (including this paragraph) then the Court must have regard to such conduct when determining costs.

2.17

It is not practicable in this protocol to address in detail how the parties might decide which method to adopt to resolve their particular dispute. However, summarised below are some of the options for resolving disputes without litigation:

- Discussion and negotiation.

- Early neutral evaluation by an independent third party (for example, a lawyer experienced in the field of personal injury or an individual experienced in the subject matter of the claim).

- Mediation – a form of facilitated negotiation assisted by an independent neutral party.

2.18

The Legal Services Commission has published a booklet on 'Alternatives to Court', CLS Direct Information Leaflet 23 (www.clsdirect.org.uk/ legalhelp/leaflet23.jsp), which lists a number of organisations that provide alternative dispute resolution services.

2.19

It is expressly recognised that no party can or should be forced to mediate or enter into any form of ADR.

Stocktake

2.20

Where a claim is not resolved when the protocol has been followed, the parties might wish to carry out a 'stocktake' of the issues in dispute, and the evidence that the court is likely to need to decide those issues, before proceedings are started. Where the defendant is insured and the pre-action steps have been conducted by the insurer, the insurer would normally be expected to nominate solicitors to act in the proceedings and the claimant's solicitor is recommended to invite the insurer to nominate solicitors to act in the proceedings and do so 7–14 days before the intended issue date.

3   THE PROTOCOL

Letter of claim

3.1

Subject to paragraph 2.10A the claimant shall send to the proposed defendant two copies of a letter of claim, immediately sufficient information is available to substantiate a realistic claim and before issues of quantum are addressed in detail. One copy of the letter is for the defendant, the second for passing on to his insurers.

3.2

The letter shall contain a clear summary of the facts on which the claim is based together with an indication of the nature of any injuries suffered and of any financial loss incurred. In cases of road traffic accidents, the letter should provide the name and address of the hospital where treatment has been obtained and the claimant's hospital reference number. Where the case is funded by a conditional fee agreement (or collective conditional fee agreement), notification should be given of the existence of the agreement and where appropriate, that there is a success fee and/or insurance premium, although not the level of the success fee or premium.

3.3

Solicitors are recommended to use a standard format for such a letter – an example is at Annex A: this can be amended to suit the particular case.

3.4

The letter should ask for details of the insurer and that a copy should be sent by the proposed defendant to the insurer where appropriate. If the insurer is known, a copy shall be sent directly to the insurer. Details of the claimant's National Insurance number and date of birth should be supplied to the defendant's insurer once the defendant has responded to the letter of claim and confirmed the identity of the insurer. This information should not be supplied in the letter of claim.

3.5

Sufficient information should be given in order to enable the defendant's insurer/solicitor to commence investigations and at least put a broad valuation on the 'risk'.

3.6

The defendant should reply within 21 calendar days of the date of posting of the letter identifying the insurer (if any) and, if necessary, identifying specifically any significant omissions from the letter of claim. If there has been no reply by the defendant or insurer within 21 days, the claimant will be entitled to issue proceedings.

3.7

The defendant('s insurers) will have a maximum of three months from the date of acknowledgment of the claim to investigate. No later than the end of that period the defendant (insurer) shall reply, stating whether liability is denied and, if so, giving reasons for their denial of liability including any alternative version of events relied upon.

3.8

Where the accident occurred outside England and Wales and/or where the defendant is outside the jurisdiction, the time periods of 21 days and three months should normally be extended up to 42 days and six months.

3.9

Where the claimant's investigation indicates that the value of the claim has increased to more than the value of the fast track limit since the letter of claim, the claimant should notify the defendant as soon as possible.

Documents

3.10

If the defendant denies liability, he should enclose with the letter of reply, documents in his possession which are material to the issues between the parties, and which would be likely to be ordered to be disclosed by the court, either on an application for pre-action disclosure, or on disclosure during proceedings.

3.11

Attached at Annex B are specimen, but non-exhaustive, lists of documents likely to be material in different types of claim. Where the claimant's investigation of the case is well advanced, the letter of claim could indicate which classes of documents are considered relevant for early disclosure. Alternatively these could be identified at a later stage.

3.12

Where the defendant admits primary liability, but alleges contributory negligence by the claimant, the defendant should give reasons supporting those allegations and disclose those documents from Annex B which are relevant to the issues in dispute. The claimant should respond to the allegations of contributory negligence before proceedings are issued.

3.13

No charge will be made for providing copy documents under the Protocol.

Special damages

3.14

The claimant will send to the defendant as soon as practicable a Schedule of Special Damages with supporting documents, particularly where the defendant has admitted liability.

Experts

3.15

Before any party instructs an expert he should give the other party a list of the name(s) of one or more experts in the relevant speciality whom he considers are suitable to instruct.

3.16

Where a medical expert is to be instructed the claimant's solicitor will organise access to relevant medical records – see specimen letter of instruction at Annex C.

3.17

Within 14 days the other party may indicate an objection to one or more of the named experts. The first party should then instruct a mutually acceptable expert (which is not the same as a joint expert). It must be emphasised that if the Claimant nominates an expert in the original letter of claim, the defendant has 14 days to object to one or more of the named experts after expiration of the period of 21 days within which he has to reply to the letter of claim, as set out in paragraph 3.6.

3.18

If the second party objects to all the listed experts, the parties may then instruct experts of their own choice. It would be for the court to decide subsequently, if proceedings are issued, whether either party had acted unreasonably.

3.19

If the second party does not object to an expert nominated, he shall not be entitled to rely on his own expert evidence within that particular speciality unless:

(a)   the first party agrees,

(b)   the court so directs, or

(c)   the first party's expert report has been amended and the first party is not prepared to disclose the original report.

3.20

Either party may send to an agreed expert written questions on the report, relevant to the issues, via the first party's solicitors. The expert should send answers to the questions separately and directly to each party.

3.21

The cost of a report from an agreed expert will usually be paid by the instructing first party: the costs of the expert replying to questions will usually be borne by the party which asks the questions.

4   REHABILITATION

4.1

The claimant or the defendant or both shall consider as early as possible whether the claimant has reasonable needs that could be met by rehabilitation treatment or other measures.

4.2

The parties shall consider, in such cases, how those needs might be addressed. The Rehabilitation Code (which is attached at Annex D) may be helpful in considering how to identify the claimant's needs and how to address the cost of providing for those needs.

4.3

The time limit set out in paragraph 3.7 *of this Protocol* shall not be shortened, except by consent to allow these issues to be addressed.

4.4

The provision of any report obtained for the purposes of assessment of provision of a party's rehabilitation needs shall not be used in any litigation arising out of the accident, the subject of the claim, save by consent and shall in any event be exempt from the provisions of paragraphs 3.15 to 3.21 inclusive of this protocol.

5   RESOLUTION OF ISSUES

5.1

Where the defendant admits liability in whole or in part, before proceedings are issued, any medical reports obtained under this protocol on which a party relies should be disclosed to the other party. The claimant should delay issuing proceedings for 21 days from disclosure of the report (unless such delay would cause his claim to become time-barred), to enable the parties to consider whether the claim is capable of settlement.

5.2

The Civil Procedure Rules Part 36 permit claimants and defendants to make offers to settle pre-proceedings. Parties should always consider before issuing if it is appropriate to make Part 36 Offer. If such an offer is made, the party making the offer must always supply sufficient evidence and/or information to enable the offer to be properly considered.

5.3

Where the defendant has admitted liability, the claimant should send to the defendant schedules of special damages and loss at least 21 days before proceedings are issued (unless that would cause the claimant's claim to become time-barred).

A   LETTER OF CLAIM

To

Defendant

Dear Sirs

Re: **Claimant's full name**

Claimant's full address

Claimant's Clock or Works Number

Claimant's Employer (name and address)

We are instructed by the above named to claim damages in connection with an *accident at work/road traffic accident/tripping accident* on   day   of   *(year)* at *(place of accident which must be sufficiently detailed to establish location)*

Please confirm the identity of your insurers. Please note that the insurers will need to see this letter as soon as possible and it may affect your insurance cover and/or the conduct of any subsequent legal proceedings if you do not send this letter to them.

The circumstances of the accident are:

(brief outline)

The reason why we are alleging fault is:

(simple explanation e.g. defective machine, broken ground)

A description of our clients' injuries is as follows:-

(brief outline)

(In cases of road traffic accidents)

Our client (state hospital reference number) received treatment for the injuries at name and address of hospital).

Our client is still suffering from the effects of his/her injury. We invite you to participate with us in addressing his/her immediate needs by use of rehabilitation.

He is employed as *(occupation)* and has had the following time off work *(dates of absence)*. His approximate weekly income is *(insert if known)*.

If you are our client's employers, please provide us with the usual earnings details which will enable us to calculate his financial loss.

We are obtaining a police report and will let you have a copy of the same upon your undertaking to meet half the fee.

We have also sent a letter of claim to *(name and address)* and a copy of that letter is attached. We understand their insurers are *(name, address and claims number if known)*.

At this stage of our enquiries we would expect the documents contained in parts *(insert appropriate parts of standard disclosure list)* to be relevant to this action.

Please note that we have entered into a conditional fee agreement with our client dated   in relation to this claim which provides for a success fee within the meaning of section 58(2) of the Courts and Legal Services Act 1990. Our client has taken out an insurance policy with [name of insurance company] of [address of insurance company] to which section 29 of the Access Justice Act 1999 applies. The policy number is   and the policy is dated   . Where the funding arrangement is an insurance policy, the party must state the name and address of the insurer, the policy number and the date of the policy, and must identify the claim or claims to which it relates (including Part 20 claims if any).

A copy of this letter is attached for you to send to your insurers. Finally we expect an acknowledgment of this letter within 21 days by yourselves or your insurers.

Yours faithfully

B PRE-ACTION PERSONAL INJURY PROTOCOL STANDARD DISCLOSURE LISTS

RTA CASES

SECTION A

In all cases where liability is at issue –

(i)   Documents identifying nature, extent and location of damage to defendant's vehicle where there is any dispute about point of impact.

(ii)   MOT certificate where relevant.

(iii)   Maintenance records where vehicle defect is alleged or it is alleged by defendant that there was an unforeseen defect which caused or contributed to the accident.

SECTION B

Accident involving commercial vehicle as defendant –

(i)   Tachograph charts or entry from individual control book.

(ii)   Maintenance and repair records required for operators' licence where vehicle defect is alleged or it is alleged by defendant that there was an unforeseen defect which caused or contributed to the accident.

SECTION C

Cases against local authorities where highway design defect is alleged –

(i)   Documents produced to comply with Section 39 of the Road Traffic Act 1988 in respect of the duty designed to promote road safety to include studies into road accidents in the relevant area and documents relating to measures recommended to prevent accidents in the relevant area.

HIGHWAY TRIPPING CLAIMS

Documents from Highway Authority for a period of 12 months prior to the accident –

(i)   Records of inspection for the relevant stretch of highway.

(ii)   Maintenance records including records of independent contractors working in relevant area.

(iii)   Records of the minutes of Highway Authority meetings where maintenance or repair policy has been discussed or decided.

(iv)   Records of complaints about the state of highways.

(v)   Records of other accidents which have occurred on the relevant stretch of highway.

WORKPLACE CLAIMS

(i)   Accident book entry.

(ii)   First aider report.

(iii)   Surgery record.

(iv)   Foreman/supervisor accident report.

(v)   Safety representatives accident report.

(vi)   RIDDOR (Reporting of Injuries, Diseases and Dangerous Occurrences Regulations) report to HSE.

(vii)   Other communications between defendants and HSE.

(viii) Minutes of Health and Safety Committee meeting(s) where accident/ matter considered.

(ix)   Report to DSS.

(x)   Documents listed above relative to any previous accident/matter identified by the claimant and relied upon as proof of negligence.

(xi)   Earnings information where defendant is employer.

Documents produced to comply with requirements of the Management of Health and Safety at Work Regulations 1992 –

(i)   Pre-accident Risk Assessment required by Regulation 3.

(ii)   Post-accident Re-Assessment required by Regulation 3.

(iii)   Accident Investigation Report prepared in implementing the requirements of Regulations 4, 6 and 9.

(iv)   Health Surveillance Records in appropriate cases required by Regulation 5.

(v)   Information provided to employees under Regulation 8.

(vi)   Documents relating to the employees health and safety training required by Regulation 11.

WORKPLACE CLAIMS – DISCLOSURE WHERE SPECIFIC REGULATIONS APPLY

SECTION A – Workplace (Health Safety and Welfare) Regulations 1992

(i)   Repair and maintenance records required by Regulation 5.

(ii)   Housekeeping records to comply with the requirements of Regulation 9.

(iii)   Hazard warning signs or notices to comply with Regulation 17 (Traffic Routes).

SECTION B – Provision and Use of Work Equipment Regulations 1998

(i) Manufacturers' specifications and instructions in respect of relevant work equipment establishing its suitability to comply with Regulation 5.

(ii) Maintenance log/maintenance records required to comply with Regulation 6.

(iii) Documents providing information and instructions to employees to comply with Regulation 8.

(iv) Documents provided to the employee in respect of training for use to comply with Regulation 9.

(v) Any notice, sign or document relied upon as a defence to alleged breaches of Regulations 14 to 18 dealing with controls and control systems.

(vi) Instruction/training documents issued to comply with the requirements of regulation 22 insofar as it deals with maintenance operations where the machinery is not shut down.

(vii) Copies of markings required to comply with Regulation 23.

(viii) Copies of warnings required to comply with Regulation 24.

SECTION C – Personal Protective Equipment at Work Regulations 1992

(i) Documents relating to the assessment of the Personal Protective Equipment to comply with Regulation 6.

(ii) Documents relating to the maintenance and replacement of Personal Protective Equipment to comply with Regulation 7.

(iii) Record of maintenance procedures for Personal Protective Equipment to comply with Regulation 7.

(iv) Records of tests and examinations of Personal Protective Equipment to comply with Regulation 7.

(v) Documents providing information, instruction and training in relation to the Personal Protective Equipment to comply with Regulation 9.

(vi) Instructions for use of Personal Protective Equipment to include the manufacturers' instructions to comply with Regulation 10.

SECTION D – Manual Handling Operations Regulations 1992

(i) Manual Handling Risk Assessment carried out to comply with the requirements of Regulation 4(1)(b)(i).

(ii) Re-assessment carried out post-accident to comply with requirements of Regulation 4(1)(b)(i).

(iii) Documents showing the information provided to the employee to give general indications related to the load and precise indications on the weight of the load and the heaviest side of the load if the centre of gravity was not positioned centrally to comply with Regulation 4(1)(b)(iii).

(iv) Documents relating to training in respect of manual handling operations and training records.

SECTION E – Health and Safety (Display Screen Equipment) Regulations 1992

(i) Analysis of work stations to assess and reduce risks carried out to comply with the requirements of Regulation 2.

(ii) Re-assessment of analysis of work stations to assess and reduce risks following development of symptoms by the claimant.

(iii) Documents detailing the provision of training including training records to comply with the requirements of Regulation 6.

(iv) Documents providing information to employees to comply with the requirements of Regulation 7.

SECTION F – Control of Substances Hazardous to Health Regulations 1999

(i) Risk assessment carried out to comply with the requirements of Regulation 6.

(ii) Reviewed risk assessment carried out to comply with the requirements of Regulation 6.

(iii) Copy labels from containers used for storage handling and disposal of carcinogenics to comply with the requirements of Regulation 7(2A)(h).

(iv) Warning signs identifying designation of areas and installations which may be contaminated by carcinogenics to comply with the requirements of Regulation 7(2A)(h).

(v) Documents relating to the assessment of the Personal Protective Equipment to comply with Regulation 7(3A).

(vi) Documents relating to the maintenance and replacement of Personal Protective Equipment to comply with Regulation 7(3A).

(vii) Record of maintenance procedures for Personal Protective Equipment to comply with Regulation 7(3A).

(viii) Records of tests and examinations of Personal Protective Equipment to comply with Regulation 7(3A).

(ix)   Documents providing information, instruction and training in relation to the Personal Protective Equipment to comply with Regulation 7(3A).

(x)   Instructions for use of Personal Protective Equipment to include the manufacturers' instructions to comply with Regulation 7(3A).

(xi)   Air monitoring records for substances assigned a maximum exposure limit or occupational exposure standard to comply with the requirements of Regulation 7.

(xii) Maintenance examination and test of control measures records to comply with Regulation 9.

(xiii) Monitoring records to comply with the requirements of Regulation 10.

(xiv) Health surveillance records to comply with the requirements of Regulation 11.

(xv)   Documents detailing information, instruction and training including training records for employees to comply with the requirements of Regulation 12.

(xvi) Labels and Health and Safety data sheets supplied to the employers to comply with the CHIP Regulations.

SECTION G – Construction (Design and Management) (Amendment) Regulations 2000

(i)   Notification of a project form (HSE F10) to comply with the requirements of Regulation 7.

(ii)   Health and Safety Plan to comply with requirements of Regulation 15.

(iii) Health and Safety file to comply with the requirements of Regulations 12 and 14.

(iv)   Information and training records provided to comply with the requirements of Regulation 17.

(v)   Records of advice from and views of persons at work to comply with the requirements of Regulation 18.

SECTION H – Pressure Systems and Transportable Gas Containers Regulations 1989

(i)   Information and specimen markings provided to comply with the requirements of Regulation 5.

(ii)   Written statements specifying the safe operating limits of a system to comply with the requirements of Regulation 7.

(iii)   Copy of the written scheme of examination required to comply with the requirements of Regulation 8.

(iv)   Examination records required to comply with the requirements of Regulation 9.

(v)   Instructions provided for the use of operator to comply with Regulation 11.

(vi)   Records kept to comply with the requirements of Regulation 13.

(vii)   Records kept to comply with the requirements of Regulation 22.

SECTION I – Lifting Operations and Lifting Equipment Regulations 1998

(i)   Record kept to comply with the requirements of Regulation 6.

SECTION J – Noise at Work Regulations 1989

(i)   Any risk assessment records required to comply with the requirements of Regulations 4 and 5.

(ii)   Manufacturers' literature in respect of all ear protection made available to claimant to comply with the requirements of Regulation 8.

(iii)   All documents provided to the employee for the provision of information to comply with Regulation 11.

SECTION K – Construction (Head Protection) Regulations 1989

(i)   Pre-accident assessment of head protection required to comply with Regulation 3(4).

(ii)   Post-accident re-assessment required to comply with Regulation 3(5).

SECTION L – The Construction (General Provisions) Regulations 1961

(i)   Report prepared following inspections and examinations of excavations etc. to comply with the requirements of Regulation 9.

SECTION M – Gas Containers Regulations 1989

(i)   Information and specimen markings provided to comply with the requirements of Regulation 5.

(ii)   Written statements specifying the safe operating limits of a system to comply with the requirements of Regulation 7.

(iii)   Copy of the written scheme of examination required to comply with the requirements of Regulation 8.

(iv)   Examination records required to comply with the requirements of Regulation 9.

(v)   Instructions provided for the use of operator to comply with Regulation 11.

C LETTER OF INSTRUCTION TO MEDICAL EXPERT

Dear Sir,

Re: *(Name and Address)*

D.O.B. –

Telephone No. –

Date of Accident –

We are acting for the above named in connection with injuries received in an accident which occurred on the above date. The main injuries appear to have been *(main injuries)*.

We should be obliged if you would examine our Client and let us have a full and detailed report dealing with any relevant pre-accident medical history, the injuries sustained, treatment received and present condition, dealing in particular with the capacity for work and giving a prognosis.

It is central to our assessment of the extent of our Client's injuries to establish the extent and duration of any continuing disability. Accordingly, in the prognosis section we would ask you to specifically comment on any areas of continuing complaint or disability or impact on daily living. If there is such continuing disability you should comment upon the level of suffering or inconvenience caused and, if you are able, give your view as to when or if the complaint or disability is likely to resolve.

Please send our Client an appointment direct for this purpose. Should you be able to offer a cancellation appointment please contact our Client direct. We confirm we will be responsible for your reasonable fees.

We are obtaining the notes and records from our Client's GP and Hospitals attended and will forward them to you when they are to hand/or please request the GP and Hospital records direct and advise that any invoice for the provision of these records should be forwarded to us.

In order to comply with Court Rules we would be grateful if you would insert above your signature a statement that the contents are true to the best of your knowledge and belief.

In order to avoid further correspondence we can confirm that on the evidence we have there is no reason to suspect we may be pursuing a claim against the hospital or its staff.

We look forward to receiving your report within _____ weeks. If you will not be able to prepare your report within this period please telephone us upon receipt of these instructions.

When acknowledging these instructions it would assist if you could give an estimate as to the likely time scale for the provision of your report and also an indication as to your fee.

Yours faithfully

D   THE 2007 REHABILITATION CODE

Introduction

The aim of this code is to promote the use of rehabilitation and early intervention in the compensation process so that the injured person makes the best and quickest possible medical, social and psychological recovery. This objective applies whatever the severity of the injuries sustained by the claimant. The Code is designed to ensure that the claimant's need for rehabilitation is assessed and addressed as a priority, and that the process of so doing is pursued on a collaborative basis by the claimant's lawyer and the compensator.

Therefore, in every case, where rehabilitation is likely to be of benefit, the earliest possible notification to the compensator of the claim and of the need for rehabilitation will be expected.

1.   Introduction

1.1   The purpose of the personal injury claims process is to put the individual back into the same position as he or she would have been in, had the accident not occurred, insofar as money can achieve that objective. The purpose of the rehabilitation code is to provide a framework within which the claimant's health, quality of life and ability to work are restored as far as possible before, or simultaneously with, the process of assessing compensation.

1.2   Although the Code is recognised by the Personal Injury Pre-Action Protocol, its provisions are not mandatory. It is recognised that the aims of the Code can be achieved without strict adherence to the terms of the Code, and therefore it is open to the parties to agree an alternative framework to achieve the early rehabilitation of the claimant.

1.3   However, the Code provides a useful framework within which claimant's lawyers and the compensator can work together to ensure that the needs of injured claimants are assessed at an early stage.

1.4   In any case where agreement on liability is not reached it is open to the parties to agree that the Code will in any event operate, and the question of delay pending resolution of liability should be balanced with the interests of the injured party. However, unless so agreed, the Code does not apply in the absence of liability or prior to agreement on liability being reached.

1.5   In this code the expression "the compensator" shall include any loss adjuster, solicitor or other person acting on behalf of the compensator.

2. The claimant's solicitor

2.1   It should be the duty of every claimant's solicitor to consider, from the earliest practicable stage, and in consultation with the claimant, the claimant's family, and where appropriate the claimant's treating physician(s), whether it is likely or possible that early intervention, rehabilitation or medical treatment would improve their present and/or long term physical and mental well being. This duty is ongoing throughout the life of the case but is of most importance in the early stages.

2.2   The claimant's solicitors will in any event be aware of their responsibilities under section 4 of the Pre-Action Protocol for Personal Injury Claims.

2.3   It shall be the duty of a claimant's solicitor to consider, with the claimant and/or the claimant's family, whether there is an immediate need for aids, adaptations, adjustments to employment to enable the claimant to keep his/her existing job, obtain suitable alternative employment with the same employer or retrain for new employment, or other matters that would seek to alleviate problems caused by disability, and then to communicate with the compensators as soon as practicable about any such rehabilitation needs, with a view to putting this Code into effect.

2.4   It shall not be the responsibility of the solicitor to decide on the need for treatment or rehabilitation or to arrange such matters without appropriate medical or professional advice.

2.5   It is the intention of this Code that the claimant's solicitor will work with the compensator to address these rehabilitation needs and that the assessment and delivery of rehabilitation needs shall be a collaborative process.

2.6   It must be recognised that the compensator will need to receive from the claimants' solicitors sufficient information for the compensator to make a proper decision about the need for intervention, rehabilitation or treatment. To this extent the claimant's solicitor must comply with the requirements of the Pre-Action Protocol to provide the compensator with full and adequate details of the injuries sustained by the claimant, the nature and extent of any or any likely continuing disability and any suggestions that may already have been made concerning the rehabilitation and/or early intervention.

2.7   There is no requirement under the Pre-Action Protocol, or under this code, for the claimant's solicitor to have obtained a full medical report. It is recognised that many cases will be identified for consideration under this code before medical evidence has actually been commissioned or obtained.

3. The Compensator

3.1 It shall be the duty of the compensator, from the earliest practicable stage in any appropriate case, to consider whether it is likely that the claimant will benefit in the immediate, medium or longer term from further medical treatment, rehabilitation or early intervention. This duty is ongoing throughout the life of the case but is most important in the early stages.

3.2 If the compensator considers that a particular claim might be suitable for intervention, rehabilitation or treatment, the compensator will communicate this to the claimant's solicitor as soon as practicable.

3.3 On receipt of such communication, the claimant's solicitor will immediately discuss these issues with the claimant and/or the claimant's family pursuant to his duty set out above.

3.4 Where a request to consider rehabilitation has been communicated by the claimant's solicitor to the compensator, it will usually be expected that the compensator will respond to such request within 21 days.

3.5 Nothing in this or any other code of practice shall in any way modify the obligations of the compensator under the Protocol to investigate claims rapidly and in any event within 3 months (except where time is extended by the claimant's solicitor) from the date of the formal claim letter. It is recognised that, although the rehabilitation assessment can be done even where liability investigations are outstanding, it is essential that such investigations proceed with the appropriate speed.

4. Assessment

4.1 Unless the need for intervention, rehabilitation or treatment has already been identified by medical reports obtained and disclosed by either side, the need for and extent of such intervention, rehabilitation or treatment will be considered by means of an assessment by an appropriately qualified person.

4.2 An assessment of rehabilitation needs may be carried out by any person or organisation suitably qualified, experienced and skilled to carry out the task. The claimant's solicitor and the compensator should endeavour to agree on the person or organisation to be chosen.

4.3 No solicitor or compensator may insist on the assessment being carried out by a particular person or organisation if [on reasonable grounds] the other party objects, such objection to be raised within 21 days from the date of notification of the suggested assessor.

4.4 The assessment may be carried out by a person or organisation which has a direct business connection with the solicitor or compensator, only if the other party agrees. The solicitor or compensator will be expected to reveal to the other party the existence of and nature of such a business connection.

5. The Assessment Process

5.1 Where possible, the agency to be instructed to provide the assessment should be agreed between the claimant's solicitor and the compensator. The method of providing instructions to that agency will be agreed between the solicitor and the compensator.

5.2 The assessment agency will be asked to carry out the assessment in a way that is appropriate to the needs of the case and, in a simple case, may include, by prior appointment, a telephone interview but in more serious cases will probably involve a face to face discussion with the claimant. The report will normally cover the following headings:-

1. The Injuries sustained by the claimant.

2. The current disability/incapacity arising from those Injuries. Where relevant to the overall picture of the claimant's needs, any other medical conditions not arising from the accident should also be separately annotated.

3. The claimant's domestic circumstances (including mobility accommodation and employment) where relevant.

4. The injuries/disability in respect of which early intervention or early rehabilitation is suggested.

5. The type of intervention or treatment envisaged.

6. The likely cost.

7. The likely outcome of such intervention or treatment.

5.3 The report should not deal with issues relating to legal liability and should therefore not contain a detailed account of the accident circumstances.

5.4 In most cases it will be expected that the assessment will take place within 14 days from the date of the letter of referral to the assessment agency.

5.5 It must be remembered that the compensator will usually only consider such rehabilitation to deal with the effects of the injuries that have been caused in the relevant accident and will normally not be expected to fund treatment for conditions which do not directly relate to the accident unless the effect of such conditions has been exacerbated by the injuries sustained in the accident.

6. The Assessment Report

6.1   The report agency will, on completion of the report, send copies onto both the claimant's solicitor and compensator simultaneously. Both parties will have the right to raise questions on the report, disclosing such correspondence to the other party.

6.2   It is recognised that for this assessment report to be of benefit to the parties, it should be prepared and used wholly outside the litigation process. Neither side can therefore, unless they agree in writing, rely on its contents in any subsequent litigation.

6.3   The report, any correspondence related to it and any notes created by the assessing agency to prepare it, will be covered by legal privilege and will not be disclosed in any legal proceedings unless the parties agree. Any notes or documents created in connection with the assessment process will not be disclosed in any litigation, and any person involved in the preparation of the report or involved in the assessment process, shall not be a compellable witness at Court. This principle is also set out in paragraph 4.4 of the Pre-Action Protocol.

6.4   The provision in paragraph 6.3 above as to treating the report etc as outside the litigation process is limited to the assessment report and any notes relating to it. Any notes and reports created during the subsequent case management process will be covered by the usual principle in relation to disclosure of documents and medical records relating to the claimant.

6.5   The compensator will pay for the report within 28 days of receipt.

6.6   This code intends that the parties will continue to work together to ensure that the rehabilitation which has been recommended proceeds smoothly and that any further rehabilitation needs are also assessed.

7. Recommendations

7.1   When the assessment report is disclosed to the compensator, the compensator will be under a duty to consider the recommendations made and the extent to which funds will be made available to implement all or some of the recommendations. The compensator will not be required to pay for intervention treatment that is unreasonable in nature, content or cost or where adequate and timely provision is otherwise available. The claimant will be under no obligation to undergo intervention, medical or investigation treatment that is unreasonable in all the circumstances of the case.

7.2   The compensator will normally be expected to respond to the claimant's solicitor within 21 days from the date upon which the assessment report is disclosed as to the extent to which the recommendations have been accepted and rehabilitation treatment would be funded and will be expected to justify, within that same timescale, any refusal to meet the cost of recommended rehabilitation.

7.3 If funds are provided by the compensator to the claimant to enable specific intervention, rehabilitation or treatment to occur, the compensator warrants that they will not, in any legal proceedings connected with the claim, dispute the reasonableness of that treatment, nor the agreed costs, provided of course that the claimant has had the recommended treatment. The compensator will not, should the claim fail or be later discontinued, or any element of contributory negligence be assessed or agreed, seek to recover from the claimant any funds that they have made available pursuant to this Code. The Rehabilitation Code is endorsed by many organisations, including:

Association of British Insurers

Association of Personal Injury Lawyers

Bodily Injury Claims Management Association

Case Management Society of the UK

Forum of Insurance Lawyers

International Underwriting Association

Motor Accident Solicitors' Society

To download the code, go to www.iua.co.uk/rehabilitationcode.

8 Starting Proceedings and Drafting Statements of Case

This chapter deals with the basic mechanics of starting court proceedings in personal injury cases and the basic principles of drafting the necessary pleadings.

8.1 General requirements

8.1.1 Claim form

Form N1 (set out at para 8.6.1) is a single claim form which can be used for one or more defendants and will contain the particulars of claim. If the particulars of claim are not served with the form, the claimant must file a copy of the claim form within 7 days of service on the defendant. The claim form must be served within 4 months (6 months if serving out of the jurisdiction).

8.1.2 Date of issue

Proceedings are started when the claim form is issued. However, for the purpose of the Limitation Act 1980, the claim is actually brought when the completed form is received by the court.

8.1.3 Required information

The claim form must contain a concise statement of the nature of the claim, specify the remedy sought, provide a statement of value and give details of whether any of the parties are acting in a representative capacity. If the particulars of claim are not served with the claim form, the claimant must state on the form that the particulars will follow. It should be noted that there is no penalty if a form of relief is not claimed on the form. The court can grant any remedy to which the claimant is entitled, irrespective of whether it is specified in the claim form, although the defendant may have an argument as to costs if he or she is forced to consider a remedy not mentioned prior to the trial. It remains essential, however, that matters such as a claim for provisional damages are specifically pleaded.

The claim form must state the amount claimed or the amount the claimant expects to recover: not more than £5,000, between £5,000 and £15,000 or more than £25,000. If it is not possible to state the amount to be recovered, this fact should be stated on the form. The claim form must state whether or not the claim for damages for personal injury (that is, the claim for damages for PLSA) exceeds £1,000.

As the claim form is a statement of case, it should be accompanied by a statement of truth (see para 8.2).

Where the claimant is a child or a person under a disability, the name should be followed by '(a child) by ... his litigation friend'.

8.2   Drafting the particulars of claim

The particulars of claim must succinctly state the facts on which the claim is based. They must also state, with grounds, any claim for aggravated, exemplary or provisional damages (see an example of particulars of claim at para 8.7).

The particulars of claim must include:

(a)   the claimant's date of birth and an outline of his or her injuries;

(b)   details of the statutory basis for the claim and the nature of the deterioration where provisional damages are claimed.

Annexed to the particulars of claim should be:

(a)   a schedule of past and future loss;

(b)   a medical report, if medical evidence is to be relied upon.

Other matters to set out in particulars of claim

Any relevant convictions of the defendant, stating the date, court convicting and the nature of the conviction and its relevance to the proceedings must be set out in the particulars of claim (section 11 of the Civil Evidence Act 1968).

Where the claimant seeks to rely on the following matters, they must also be set out in the particulars of claim:

(a)   any allegation of fraud;

(b)   the fact of any illegality;

(c)   details of any misrepresentation;

(d)   details of all breaches of trust;

(e)   notice or knowledge of a fact;

(f)   details of unsoundness of mind or undue influence;

(g)   details of wilful default;

(h)   any facts relating to mitigation of loss or damage.

The particulars of claim must be accompanied by a statement of truth and must display the case number, title of proceedings and the claimant's address for service.

Statement of truth

This consists of a statement that the party presenting the claim believes the facts to be true. It must be signed by the party or his solicitor.

Claim for interest

If the claim is also for interest, the particulars of claim must state the grounds on which this is being claimed. In a claim for a specific sum of money, the percentage rate must be stated, as well as the date from which interest is claimed, the amount calculated and the subsequent daily rate.

Fatal accident claims

The particulars of claim must state that the claim is brought under the Fatal Accidents Act 1976 and detail the dependants on whose part the claim is brought and the nature of their claim.

Optional inclusions in particulars of claim

These comprise: points of law which may be relied on, names of witnesses and supporting documents such as expert reports.

Schedule of damages

The particulars of claim must be accompanied by a schedule of damages which sets out the details of the past and future expenses and losses. In simple cases this can be a short document. In complex cases the schedule will have to set out full details of matters such as future loss of earnings, care needs and accommodation needs.

Service

Once issued, the claim, along with forms for the defendant to use for admitting or defending the claim and acknowledging the service, must be served within 4 months (see Form N9 at para 8.6.2). If a solicitor has been nominated to accept service, then service must take place on the nominated solicitor. Service on the defendant after a solicitor has been nominated is not good service, unless the defendant is a limited company. Similarly, service on the defendant's insurance company is not normally good service.

Failure to serve properly is a common ground of problems and negligence claims against solicitors. Ensuring that service takes place on the appropriate person, at the appropriate address and within the appropriate time period is of critical importance. These are not matters that should be delegated.

8.3   Responding to claim

8.3.1   Defendant's options

Under the CPR, a defendant has a number of options when served with a claim form. He or she can:

(a)   serve an admission in accordance with CPR Part 14;

(b)   serve a defence in accordance with CPR Part 15;

(c)   serve a defence and a partial admission;

(d)   file an acknowledgment of service.

8.3.2   Acknowledgment of service

This can be served in two circumstances:

(a)   where the defendant cannot file a defence within 14 days of service of particulars of claim – filing an acknowledgment effectively gives him or her an extra 14 days (the time for service of defence then being 28 days after service);

(b)   where a defendant wishes to dispute the court's jurisdiction (in which case, the defendant must indicate on the acknowledgement of service that jurisdiction is disputed).

Content

The defendant's name should be set out in full and his or her address for service must be given.

The acknowledgment should be signed either by the defendant or by his or her legal representative.

Withdrawal

An acknowledgment of service may only be withdrawn or amended with the court's permission.

Admission

A party may admit the whole or part of a claim by giving written notice. Where the claim is not for money, only the claimant may apply for judgment. Such a judgment will be that which appears to the court to be warranted by the admission.

8.3.3   Defence

Drafting defence and/or counterclaim

The defendant in his or her defence must state which of the allegations he or she denies, which he or she is unable to admit or deny but which he or she requires the claimant to prove and which allegations he or she admits (see an example of a defence at para 8.7; alternatively, Form N9D at para 8.6.3 can be used).

Where the defendant admits an allegation, the defence must state the reasons for doing so and, if the defendant intends to put forward a different version of events to the claimant, he or she must state his or her own version.

Where a defendant *fails* to deal with the allegation, but has set out in his or her defence the nature of his or her case regarding the issue to which the allegation is relevant, it shall be taken to be required that the allegation be proved by the claimant.

The defendant must specifically plead:

(a)   contributory negligence;

(b)   denials that the defendant has been convicted as alleged or allegations that the conviction is irrelevant or erroneous.

Pleading limitation

If the defence is relying on a limitation period, the defence must set out the details of the expiry of the limitation period. A general assertion that the action is statute barred is not sufficient.

Statement of truth

The defence must be verified by a statement of truth.

Disputing jurisdiction and proper service of claim form

A defendant may wish to argue that the court does not have jurisdiction, either because the accident happened abroad or because the claim form has been incorrectly served. In these cases, it is essential that the only steps that the defendant takes are:

(a)   to file the acknowledgement of service   indicating that the defendant intends to dispute jurisdiction;

(b)   to issue an application under CPR Part 11 disputing the court's jurisdiction within 14 days of the acknowledgment.

It is important to note that these rules relating to jurisdiction cover cases where the defendant is arguing that the claim form has been incorrectly served or an extension of time for service of the claim form has been wrongly granted. Making any other application will mean that the defendant has accepted that the court has jurisdiction (*Hoddinott v Persimmon Homes (Wessex) Ltd* [2007] EWCA Civ 1203, [2008] 1 WLR 806).

Responding to medical report

When the particulars of claim are accompanied by a medical report, the defendant must state in the defence whether he or she agrees, disputes or neither agrees nor disputes but has no knowledge of the matter set out in the medical report.

Where the defendant disputes any part of the medical report, his or her reasons for doing so must be set out in the defence.

If the defendant has obtained his or her own medical report on which the defence intends to rely, the report must be attached to the defence.

Responding to schedule of loss

When a schedule of loss accompanies the claim form, the defendant should include in the defence or in a separate document the counter-schedule stating which items he or she agrees, disputes or neither agrees nor disputes but has no knowledge of. When any item is disputed, the defence should include an alternative figure where appropriate.

Statement of value

It is a mandatory requirement that the claimant provide such a statement. When the defence disputes that statement, it must state why and give its own statement of value.

Counterclaims

The defendant makes a counterclaim against the claimant by filing the particulars of the counterclaim. The court's permission is not required where the counterclaim is served with the defence. A counterclaim may be filed at any other time with the court's permission.

Any counterclaim should be in the same document, immediately after the defence. If it relates to the same incident, it is *usually* sufficient to refer back to the allegations in the defence. Otherwise, the negligence or other wrong by the claimant must be alleged and particulars given.

The defendant must allege that the claimant's wrongful act has caused loss and give particulars of such loss. The defendant claims interest on damages under section 69 of the County Courts Act 1984.

8.4   Reply and/or defence to counterclaim

8.4.1   Are they necessary?

It is never mandatory to serve a reply since the claimant is deemed to deny allegations in the defence. However, a reply may be necessary to deal with points not covered in the statement of claim, for example, contributory negligence.

A claimant who files a reply to a defence but fails to deal with the matter raised in the defence shall be taken to require that matter to be proved.

The reply must be verified by a statement of truth.

Pleadings may still be filed after the reply but to do this the permission of the court must be obtained.

A defence to counterclaim should be filed to prevent the defendant applying for judgment on the counterclaim.

8.4.2   Notice to insurers

If the claimant is insured, the insurers should be notified of any counterclaim or they might be able to repudiate liability to meet it. They should also be asked whether they wish the claimant's solicitors to act for them on the counterclaim.

8.5   Key points

- There are important mandatory requirements for both the claim form and the particulars of claim.

- A schedule of damages must accompany the particulars of claim.

- If the defendant wishes to defend the claim, he or she must send out both an acknowledgment of service stating that the claim is to be defended and the defence. The defence should also respond to the claimant's schedule of damages.

8.6   Forms

The following forms are reproduced in full below:

8.6.1 Claim form (N1)

Claim Form

Click here to clear your data after printing

In the	
	for court use only
Claim No.	
Issue date	

Claimant

SEAL

Defendant(s)

Brief details of claim

Value

Defendant's name and address			Amount claimed	
			Court fee	
			Solicitor's costs	
			Total amount	

£

The court office at

is open between 10 am and 4 pm Monday to Friday. When corresponding with the court, please address forms or letters to the Court Manager and quote the claim number.

N1 Claim form (CPR Part 7) (01.02)   *Printed on behalf of The Court Service*

	Claim No.	

Does, or will, your claim include any issues under the Human Rights Act 1998? ☐ Yes ☐ No

Particulars of Claim (attached)(to follow)

Statement of Truth
*(I believe)(The Claimant believes) that the facts stated in these particulars of claim are true.
* I am duly authorised by the claimant to sign this statement

Full name _____

Name of claimant's solicitor's firm _____

signed _____   position or office held _____
*(Claimant)(Litigation friend)(Claimant's solicitor)   (if signing on behalf of firm or company)
*delete as appropriate

Claimant's or claimant's solicitor's address to which documents or payments should be sent if different from overleaf including (if appropriate) details of DX, fax or e-mail.

8.6.2 Response pack (N9)

	Click here to reset form	Click here to print form

Response pack

You should read the 'notes for defendant' attached to the claim form which will tell you when and where to send the forms

Included in this pack are:

- either **Admission Form N9A** (if the claim is for a specified amount)
- or **Admission Form N9C** (if the claim is for an unspecified amount or is not a claim for money)

- either **Defence and Counterclaim Form N9B** (if the claim is for a specified amount)
- or **Defence and Counterclaim Form N9D** (if the claim is for an unspecified amount or is not a claim for money)

- **Acknowledgment of service** (see below)

	Complete
If you admit the claim or the amount claimed and/or you want time to pay	the admission form
If you admit part of the claim	the admission form and the defence form
If you dispute the whole claim or wish to make a claim (a counterclaim) against the claimant	the defence form
If you need 28 days (rather than 14) from the date of service to prepare your defence, or wish to contest the court's jurisdiction	the acknowledgment of service
If you do nothing, judgment may be entered against you	

- -

Acknowledgment of service

Defendant's full name if different from the name given on the claim form

Name of court	
Claim No.	
Claimant (including ref.)	
Defendant	

Address to which documents about this claim should be sent (including reference if appropriate)

	If applicable
Telephone no.	
Fax no.	
DX no.	
Postcode	Your ref.

E-mail

Tick the appropriate box

1. I intend to defend all of this claim ☐
2. I intend to defend part of this claim ☐
3. I intend to contest jurisdiction ☐

(My) (Defendant's) date of birth is ☐☐/☐☐/☐☐☐☐

If you file an acknowledgment of service but do not file a defence within 28 days of the date of service of the claim form, or particulars of claim if served separately, judgment may be entered against you.

If you do not file an application to dispute the jurisdiction of the court within 14 days of the date of filing this acknowledgment of service, it will be assumed that you accept the court's jurisdiction and judgment may be entered against you.

If served outside the jurisdiction see CPR rule 6.35 and 6.37(5).

Signed

(Defendant) (Defendant's solicitor) (Litigation friend)

Position or office held (if signing on behalf of firm or company)

Date ☐☐/☐☐/☐☐☐☐

The court office at

is open between 10 am and 4 pm Monday to Friday. When corresponding with the court, please address forms or letters to the Court Manager and quote the claim number.

N9 Response pack (10.08)

© Crown copyright 2008

8.6.3 Defence and counterclaim (N9D)

Defence and Counterclaim (unspecified amount, non-money and return of goods claims)	Click here to reset form | Click here to print form Name of court
	Claim No.
• Fill in this form if you wish to dispute all or part of the claim and/or make a claim against the claimant (a counterclaim) • You have a limited number of days to complete and return this form to the court.	Claimant (including ref.)
• Before completing this form, please read the notes for guidance attached to the claim form. • Please ensure that all the boxes at the top right of this form are completed. You can obtain the correct names and number from the claim form. The court cannot trace your case without this information.	Defendant

• Fill in this form if you wish to dispute all or part of the claim and/or make a claim against the claimant (a counterclaim)
• You have a limited number of days to complete and return this form to the court.
• Before completing this form, please read the notes for guidance attached to the claim form.
• Please ensure that all the boxes at the top right of this form are completed. You can obtain the correct names and number from the claim form. The court cannot trace your case without this information.

How to fill in this form
• Set out your defence in section 1. If necessary continue on a separate piece of paper making sure that the claim number is clearly shown on it. In your defence you must state which allegations in the particulars of claim you deny and your reasons for doing so. If you fail to deny an allegation it may be taken that you admit it.
• If you dispute only some of the allegations you must
  - specify which you admit and which you deny; and
  - give your own version of events if different from the claimant's.
• If the claim is for money and you dispute the claimant's statement of value, you must say why and if possible give your own statement of value.

• If you wish to make a claim against the claimant (a counterclaim) complete section 2
• Complete and sign section 3 before returning this form.

Where to send this form
• send or take this form immediately to the court at the address given on the claim form.
• Keep a copy of the claim form and the defence form.

Need help with your legal problems?
Community legal advice is a free confidential service, funded by legal aid. They can help you find the information and advice you need by putting you in touch with relevant agencies, helplines or local advice services. And if you are eligible for legal aid, the service can offer specialist legal advice over the telephone in cases involving: debt; housing; employment; benefits, and education
Call **0845 345 4 345** or **www.communitylegaladvice.org.uk**

1. Defence

(continue over the page)

Claim No.	

Defence (continued)

2. If you wish to make a claim against the claimant (a counterclaim)

- To start your counterclaim, you will have to pay a fee. Court staff can tell you how much you have to pay.
- You may not be able to make a counterclaim where the claimant is the Crown (e.g. a Government Department). Ask at your local county court office for further information.

If your claim is for a specific sum of money, how much are you claiming? £

I enclose the counterclaim fee of £

My claim is for *(please specify nature of claim)*

What are your reasons for making the counterclaim?
If you need to continue on a separate sheet put the claim number in the top right hand corner.

3. Signed - To be signed by you or by your solicitor or litigation friend.

*(I believe) (The defendant believes) that the facts stated in this form are true.
*I am duly authorised by the defendant to sign this statement.

Position or office held
(If signing on behalf of firm or company)

delete as appropriate

Date ☐☐ / ☐☐ / ☐☐☐☐

Defendant's date of birth, if an individual ☐☐ / ☐☐ / ☐☐☐☐

Give an address to which notices about this case can be sent to you

	If applicable
	Telephone no.
	Fax no.
Postcode ☐☐☐☐ ☐☐☐	DX no.

E-mail

Click here to print form

8.7   Draft particulars of claim and defence

IN THE LUDDENDEN COUNTY COURT   CASE NO: CX2399239
BETWEEN:

MR SIMON PAINLESS

Claimant

–and–

MR MARCUS CONWOW

Defendant

PARTICULARS OF CLAIM

1.   On 1 December 2010 at about 8.00 am the Claimant was driving his motor cycle registration number SP 1 along the High Street in Luddenden and had stopped at the junction with Cow Lane.

2.   The Claimant was intending to turn right into Cow Lane and was stationary with his right hand indicator flashing.

3.   A Ford Cortina motor car registration number RAM 1 owned and driven by the Defendant was proceeding along Cow Lane.

4.   The Defendant's car turned right into the High Street and collided with the Claimant's motor cycle.

5.   The collision was caused by the negligence of the Defendant.

PARTICULARS OF NEGLIGENCE

The Defendant was negligent in that he:

(a)   cut the corner;

(b)   failed to indicate that he was about to turn right;

(c)   drove onto the wrong side of the road;

(d)   failed to apply his brakes and steering in time or at all so as to steer or control his motor car so as to avoid driving into the Claimant;

(e)   failed to keep any proper look out and/or to observe the presence of the Claimant;

(f)   drove into collision with the Claimant's vehicle.

6. The Claimant will rely on the fact that on 1 March 2011 the Defendant was convicted at Luddenden Magistrates' Court of careless driving. The conviction is relevant in that it arose out of the happening of the said accident. A plea of guilty was entered, where upon the Defendant was fined £100 and incurred four penalty points.

7. As a result of the Defendant's negligence the Claimant, who was born on 1 April 1978, has suffered pain, injury, loss and damage.

PARTICULARS OF INJURY

[Note: a medical report should also be served with the Particulars of Claim]

(a) Colles fracture of right wrist

(b) Compound fracture of left femur

(c) Bruising and grazing to the left elbow and thigh

(d) The Claimant has been unable to resume his hobby of shark fishing.

PARTICULARS OF SPECIAL DAMAGE

[Note: a schedule of special damages should also accompany the Particulars of Claim]

(a)	Loss of earnings from 1 December 2010	
	(particularised in schedule served herewith)	£2,800
(b)	Value of motor cycle damaged beyond repair	£750
(c)	Value of clothing damaged beyond repair	
	(particularised in schedule)	£325
(d)	Travelling expenses to and from hospital	£108
(e)	Prescriptions	£42
		£4,025

8. Further, pursuant to s 69 of the County Courts Act 1984 the Claimant is entitled to and claims to recover interest on the amount found to be due at such rate and for such period as the Court thinks fit.

STATEMENT OF TRUTH

*(I believe)(The Claimant believes) that the facts stated in these Particulars of Claim are true.

*I am duly authorised by the Claimant to sign this statement

Full name: Joe Bloggs

Name of claimant's solicitor's firm: Hugo Fable & Co

Signed:

*(Claimant)(Litigation friend)(Claimant's solicitor)

*delete as appropriate

Hugo Fable & Co, Tenure Building, University Street, Luddenden

Solicitor for the Claimant

IN THE LUDDENDEN COUNTY COURT   CASE NO: CX2399239

BETWEEN:

MR SIMON PAINLESS

Claimant

–and–

MR MARCUS CONWOW

Defendant

DEFENCE

1. The Defendant admits that on the date and at the place mentioned in the Particulars of Claim a collision occurred between a motor cycle driven by the Claimant and a motor car driven by the Defendant. In all other particulars paragraphs 1, 2, 3 and 4 are denied. The collision happened when the Claimant pulled out in front of the Defendant making a collision inevitable.

2. The Defendant denies that he was thereby guilty of the alleged or any negligence or that the said negligence was caused as alleged in paragraph 5 of the Particulars of Claim. The accident occurred as a result of the negligence of the Claimant in pulling out in front of the Defendant's vehicle.

3. The Defendant admits the conviction of careless driving as alleged in paragraph 6 of the Particulars of Claim. It is denied that the conviction is relevant to the issues herein, the conviction was erroneous.

4. Further and/or in the alternative the collision was caused solely, or alternatively contributed to, by the negligence of the Claimant.

PARTICULARS OF NEGLIGENCE

The Claimant was negligent in that he:

(a)   pulled out in front of the Defendant's vehicle.

(b)   drove too fast;

(c)   failed to keep a proper look out;

(d)   failed to indicate his intention of turning right into Cow Lane;

(e)   continued to turn into Cow Lane when he saw or should have seen the Defendant's vehicle about to turn into his path;

(f)   drove in front of the Defendant's vehicle;

(g)   failed to slow down, stop, swerve or take such other action as was necessary to avoid the said collision.

5.   No admissions are made as to the alleged or any pain, injury, loss or damage or as to any entitlement to interest. The Claimant does not admit or deny the contents of the Claimant's medical report. A counter-schedule of damages is served herewith.

STATEMENT OF TRUTH

*I believe)(The Defendant believes) that the facts stated in this Defence are true.

*I am duly authorised by the Defendant to sign this statement

Full name: Joe Bloggs

Name of Defendant's solicitor's firm: Gradgrind & Co

Signed:

*(Claimant)(Litigation Friend)(Claimant's solicitor)

*delete as appropriate

Gradgrind & Co, 14 Fowler Street, Luddenden

Solicitor for the Defendant

9 Drafting Witness Statements and Use of Expert Witnesses

In many cases, the witness statement will be the only chance that a party, or witness, has to address the court. It is common for the court not to allow supplementary questions or elaboration of witness statements.

The drafting of the witness statement is isolated here because it is an essential part of the personal injury process that is often overlooked. It is extremely difficult, at trial, to repair the damage caused by bad witness statements. Further, witness statements can create insurmountable problems and lose a case, whereas effective witness statements can serve to win the case.

9.1 Rules relating to the drafting of witness statements

The rules relating to witness statements are in CPR Part 32 and are supplemented by a very important Practice Direction – CPR Practice Direction 32.

9.1.1 Form of witness statement

Paragraph 17 of Practice Direction 32 states:

17.1

The witness statement should be headed with the title of the proceedings ... where the proceedings are between several parties with the same status it is [possible to truncate the headings] ...

17.2

At the top right hand corner of the first page there should be clearly written:

(1) the party on whose behalf it is made,

(2) the initials and surname of the witness,

(3) the number of the statement in relation to that witness,

(4) the identifying initials and number of each exhibit referred to, and

(5) the date the statement was made.

9.1.2   Body of witness statement

Paragraph 18 of Practice Direction 32 states:

18.1

The witness statement must, if practicable, be in the intended witness's own words, the statement should be expressed in the first person and should also state:

(1) the full name of the witness,

(2) his place of residence or, if he is making the statement in his professional, business or other occupational capacity, the address at which he works, the position he holds and the name of his firm or employer,

(3) his occupation, or if he has none, his description, and

(4) the fact that he is a party to the proceedings or is the employee of such a party if it be the case.

18.2

A witness statement must indicate:

(1) which of the statements in it are made from the witness's own knowledge and which are matters of information or belief, and

(2) the source for any matters of information or belief.

18.3

An exhibit used in conjunction with a witness statement should be verified and identified by the witness and remain separate from the witness statement.

18.4

Where a witness refers to an exhibit or exhibits he should state 'I refer to the (*description of exhibit*) marked ...'.

18.5

The provisions of paragraphs 11.3 to 15.3 (exhibits) apply similarly to witness statements as they do to affidavits.

18.6

Where a witness makes more than one witness statement to which there are exhibits, in the same proceedings, the numbering of the exhibits should run consecutively throughout and not start again with each witness statement.

9.1.3   Format of witness statements

It is important that litigators are aware of the precise format required of witness statements (a failure to comply with the requirements can lead to the evidence not being admitted or the costs of preparation being disallowed). Paragraphs 19 and 20 of Practice Direction 32 state:

19.1

A witness statement should:

(1) be produced on durable quality A4 paper with a 3.5cm margin,

(2) be fully legible and should normally be typed on one side of the paper only,

(3) where possible, be bound securely in a manner which would not hamper filing, or otherwise each page should be endorsed with the case number and should bear the initials of the witness,

(4) have the pages numbered consecutively as a separate statement (or one of several statements contained in a file),

(5) be divided into numbered paragraphs,

(6) have all numbers, including dates, expressed in figures, and

(7) give in the margin the reference to any document or documents mentioned.

19.2

It is usually convenient for a witness statement to follow the chronological sequence of the events or matters dealt with, each paragraph of a witness statement should as far as possible be confined to a distinct portion of the subject.

Statement of Truth

20.1

A witness statement is the equivalent of the oral evidence which the witness would, if called, give in his evidence; it must include a statement by the intended witness that he believes the facts in it are true.

20.2

To verify a witness statement the statement of truth is as follows:

'I believe that the facts stated in this witness statement are true.'

20.3

Attention is drawn to rule 32.14 which sets out the consequences of verifying a witness statement containing a false statement without an honest belief in its truth.

The basic point for present purposes is that the *structure* of the statement must be correct. A statement that does not comply with the rules may not be admitted and, due to no fault of the witness, may be given less weight.

9.2 Use of precedents

Individual styles of drafting vary; however, it is important that:

(a) the statements are in a logical order with numbered paragraphs;

(b) all the matters that the party needs to establish (or disprove) are dealt with.

So, for instance, a witness statement drafted on behalf of a claimant could have a simple template:

• Who I am.

• The facts of the accident.

• Why the accident was the defendant's fault.

• The injuries I suffered.

• The losses I have suffered.

9.3 Preparation for drafting

9.3.1 Read the statements of case

Know what is in issue, particularly any positive allegations, contributory negligence and failure to mitigate loss.

9.3.2 Read the documents

Have all the defendant's documents been seen? Are there any that present any real difficulties? Can these difficulties be explained?

9.3.3 Go back to basics

Think again about what needs to be achieved. How does each sentence in the witness statement progress towards this? Is there any unnecessary material (eg personal abuse) that can – and should – be excluded?

9.4 Warning clients and witnesses of the importance of statement of truth

It is important that clients and witnesses are told that the statements they make are important legal documents and that they must check the truth and accuracy of the statements before they sign them. Signing a statement that is untrue or inaccurate could amount to a contempt of court.

9.5 Expert witnesses

The claimant must serve a doctor's report with the particulars of claim. The procedure by which this report is obtained is set out at para 7.5.2. However, the claimant cannot rely on this report at trial without permission of the court. CPR rule 35.4 states that no party can call an expert or use an expert's report as evidence without the court's approval.

The court's duty is to restrict expert evidence to that which is reasonably required to resolve the proceedings (CPR rule 35.1).

A party applying for permission to call expert evidence must identify the field in which expert evidence is required and, where practicable, the name of the proposed expert. The report must be given in written form.

The court has power to appoint a single joint expert (CPR rule 35.7).

9.5.1 Duty of expert

The expert's duty is to help the court on matters within his or her area of expertise. This duty overrides any obligation the expert has to those who instructed him or her (CPR rule 35.3). The form of an expert's report is set out in Practice Direction 35.

9.5.2 Written questions to expert

The parties can put written questions to an expert appointed by another party or a single joint expert. These must be put within 28 days of service of the expert's report or with the permission of the court (CPR rule 35.6).

9.5.3 Use by one party of expert's report disclosed by another

Where one party has disclosed an expert's report, any party may use that expert's report as evidence at the trial (CPR rule 35.11).

9.5.4   Discussions between experts

The court can order a discussion between experts to identify and discuss the expert issues in the proceedings and attempt to reach agreement. Where a discussion takes place between experts, the court can direct that the experts prepare a statement setting out the matters on which they agree and, where they disagree, the reasons for disagreeing. Where experts reach agreement in such discussions, such an agreement does not bind the parties unless the parties expressly agree to be bound by it (**CPR** rule 35.12).

9.6   Key points

- There are important rules relating to the form of witness statements.

- The witness statement must be in the witness's own words.

- The witness must be warned that the statement is a legal document and told to check the truth and accuracy of the statement prior to signature.

- The parties need permission of the court to adduce expert evidence and call expert evidence at trial. The court can appoint a single joint expert.

- The expert's duty is to the court.

- The parties can put questions to the expert.

- The court can order a joint meeting of experts to ascertain matters upon which they agree and the reasons for any disagreement.

10 Part 36 Offers, Part 20 Proceedings and Interim Payments

This chapter deals with three major tactics available to a defendant: payments into court, Part 20 proceedings and the claimant's tactic of interim payments.

10.1 Offers to settle (CPR Part 36)

The courts are keen to promote settlement where possible. Both parties can make offers to settle. Form N242A at para 10.5.1 may be used, although this is not a necessity.

10.1.1 Purpose of Part 36 offers

To counter the powerful weapon of the costs of legal proceedings, the defendant may, at any time before or after the commencement of proceedings but before judgment, without admitting liability make a Part 36 offer to settle the claim. The offer can be in relation to liability (for instance, making an offer of contributory negligence) or in relation to damages (offering a specific amount).

10.1.2 Claimant's Part 36 offer to settle

A claimant may make a Part 36 offer to settle. An offer to settle made before the commencement of proceedings may be taken into account when making any order as to costs. The offer can be in relation to liability or damages.

10.1.3 Interest and offer

An offer is presumed to be inclusive of interest until the date on which the offer expires (CPR rule 36.3(3)).

10.1.4 Consequences of Part 36 offer when offer accepted

Where a claimant accepts a Part 36 offer from the defendant, the claimant is entitled to his or her costs of the action on the standard basis.

Similarly, where the defendant accepts the claimant's Part 36 offer, the claimant is entitled to the costs of the proceedings up to the date when the defendant serves notice of acceptance.

10.1.5 Where defendant does not accept claimant's Part 36 offer and claimant does better at trial

Where the claimant does better than his or her proposed Part 36 offer, the court may order interest on the whole or part of the sum at a rate not higher than 10% above base rate. The court may also order that the claimant is entitled to costs on an indemnity basis from the date the defendant could have accepted the offer without needing the court's permission and award interest on those costs at a rate not exceeding 10% above base rate.

10.1.6 Where claimant does not accept defendant's Part 36 offer and fails to do better at trial

Where the claimant fails to do better than the Part 36 offer, he or she is liable to pay the defendant's costs of the action from the latest day on which the claimant could have accepted the offer. Further, the claimant will not be able to recover from the defendant for the costs he or she has incurred during this period.

10.1.7 Tactical considerations

A carefully calculated Part 36 offer is an important tactical defence weapon since the costs risk puts great pressure on the claimant to settle for less than might be received at a trial. The best defence tactic is probably to make the offer in the action, to maximise the risk of later costs, and to make one, or at the most two payments (to make more smacks of weakness). The payment must be sufficiently large as to put real doubt into the mind of the claimant's advisers that it is likely to be beaten at the trial, while offering a real saving to the defendant.

Because of these risks, the claimant's solicitors must advise the client carefully both orally and in writing and, in a substantial case, obtain counsel's advice.

Whilst the consequences for a defendant who fails to beat an offer are not as grave as they are for the claimant, it is clear that a defendant must consider a claimant's offer seriously. The additional interest and indemnity costs could have a major effect on the overall sum that the defendant has to pay.

10.1.8 Procedure: formal requirements of Part 36 offer

Offers made before proceedings are issued

If a party makes an offer to settle before proceedings begin which complies with CPR Part 36, then the court will take into account that offer when assessing costs.

The offer must:

(a) be expressed to remain open for at least 21 days after the date on which it was made;

(b) include an offer to pay the costs of the offeree up to the date 21 days after it was made, if made by a potential defendant to the action; and

(c) otherwise comply with the requirements of CPR Part 36.

Offers made after issue of proceedings

Where the offer is in an action where there is a claim for future financial loss, the offer must state the amount of the lump sum that the party is offering to pay or accept. If the party is offering to pay, or accept, periodical payments, the amount and duration of those payments must be stated together with what retail price index each payment is to be varied by.

Where there is a claim for provisional damages, the Part 36 offer must specify whether the offeror is proposing that the settlement should include an award of provisional damages, what the lump sum is and the period for which it is proposed that the claimant can make a further application for damages should the medical condition deteriorate (for a discussion of periodical payments and provisional damages, see para 3.8) (CPR rule 36.5).

Where the case is one in which a payment has to be made to the CRU (see para 3.10.3), the Part 36 offer has to state the amount of the gross compensation, the name and amount of any deductible benefit by which the gross amount is reduced and the net amount of compensation (CPR rule 36.15(6)).

10.1.9   Offers made to minors and protected parties

Where a party is a minor or a protected party any Part 36 offer made cannot be accepted without approval of the court (CPR rule 21.10(1)).

10.1.10   Withdrawal of offers

A Part 36 offer remains open until withdrawn even if a counter offer is made (*Gibbon v Manchester City Council* [2010] EWCA Civ 726). If a party wants to make an offer that expires a number of days after it is made, this should be made absolutely clear. An offer which purports to be a Part 36 offer will not readily be interpreted as a time-limited offer and it will remain open until a formal notice of withdrawal is made (*C v D* [2011] EWCA Civ 646).

10.2   Part 20 proceedings – joining new parties in an action

CPR Part 20 deals with:

(a)   a counterclaim by a defendant against the claimant or against the claimant and some other person;

(b)   a *claim* by a defendant against any person (whether or not he or she is already a party) for contribution, indemnity or some other remedy.

If the defendant wishes to counterclaim against a person other than the claimant, he or she must apply to the court for an order that that person be joined as a defendant to the counterclaim. This application can be made without notice and, when making the order, the court will make case management directions. A defendant who has filed an acknowledgement of service or a defence can make a Part 20 claim for contribution or indemnity against another defendant by filing a notice containing a statement of the nature of the grounds of his claim and serving notice on the other defendant.

10.2.1   Other Part 20 claims

If the Part 20 claim is not a counterclaim or a claim for contribution or indemnity from a co-defendant then:

(a)   the Part 20 claim is made when the court issues a Part 20 claim form;

(b)   the defendant can make a Part 20 claim without the court's permission if the Part 20 claim is issued before or at the same time as he or she files the defence;

(c) the defendant can make a Part 20 claim at any other time, but needs the court's permission. An application for permission to make a Part 20 claim can be made without notice unless the court directs otherwise;

(d) particulars of the Part 20 claim must be contained in or served with a Part 20 claim.

10.2.2 Title of proceedings

The title of every Part 20 claim must include:

(a) the full name of each party;

(b) each party's status in the proceedings.

10.2.3 Procedure for serving Part 20 claim form on non-party

When serving a Part 20 claim on a person who is not already a party, it must be accompanied by:

(a) a form for defending the claim;

(b) a form for admitting the claim;

(c) a form for acknowledgement of service; and

(d) a copy of every statement of case which has already been served in the proceedings and such other documents as the court may direct.

10.2.4 Part 20 hearing

It should not be taken for granted that the Part 20 claim will automatically be heard with the first claim. The court has the power to order that matters be dealt with separately and to decide the order in which matters are tried. This will be considered at any case management conference and the court must have regard to:

(a) the connection between the Part 20 claim and the claim made by the claimant against the defendant;

(b) whether the Part 20 claimant is seeking substantially the same remedy which some other party is claiming from him or her; and

(c) whether the Part 20 claimant wants the court to decide any question connected with the subject matter of proceedings:

(i)   not only between existing parties but also between existing parties and a person not already an existing party; or

(ii)   against an existing party not only in a capacity in which he or she is already a party but also in some further capacity.

10.2.5   Judgment in default on Part 20 claims

Special rules apply where the Part 20 claim is not a counterclaim or a claim by a defendant for an indemnity or contribution against another defendant. If the party against whom the Part 20 claim is made fails to file an acknowledgement of service or a defence in respect of the Part 20 claim, he or she is deemed to admit the Part 20 claim and is bound by any decision or judgment in the main proceedings insofar as it is relevant to any matter arising in the Part 20 claim. Further, if default judgment is given against the Part 20 claimant, it is possible to obtain default judgment on a Part 20 claim. The Part 20 claimant can obtain judgment by filing a request. However, the Part 20 claimant cannot enter judgment without the court's permission if:

(a)   the claimant has not satisfied the default judgment which has been given against him or her;

(b)   the claimant wishes to obtain judgment for any remedy other than a contribution or indemnity.

However, an application for the court's permission can be made without notice unless the court otherwise directs.

10.3   Interim payments

10.3.1   Purpose of interim payments

Interim payments are payments on account of any damages which defendants may be ordered to pay. They are designed to meet the complaint that claimants with strong cases often have to wait long periods before receiving any compensation, for example, because their medical position has not yet stabilised. Claimants' solicitors should consider applying for interim payments since they can greatly reduce any financial hardship claimants may be suffering (though they are not limited to such cases). Interim payments may also be a means of financing claimants' cases (see Chapter 5).

10.3.2   Procedural points

The important procedural points are that:

(a)   the claimant cannot apply for an order for an interim payment before the end of the period for filing an acknowledgement of service by the defendant against whom the application is made;

(b)   the claimant can make more than one application for an order for an interim payment;

(c)   a copy of the application notice for an order for an interim payment must be served at least 14 days before the hearing of the application and must be supported by evidence;

(d)   if the respondent to the application wishes to rely on written evidence, this must be filed and served on every other party to the application at least 7 days before the application. The claimant must then file evidence in reply at least 3 days before the hearing.

10.3.3   Evidence in support

An application for an interim payment must be supported by evidence dealing with:

(a)   the sum of money sought by way of an interim payment;

(b)   the items or matters in respect of which the interim payment is sought;

(c)   the sum of money for which final judgment is likely to be given;

(d)   establishing the reasons for believing that the requisites for obtaining an interim payment;

(e)   any other relevant matters;

(f)   details of special damages and past and future loss;

(g)   in a claim under the Fatal Accidents Act 1976, details of the person on whose behalf the claim is made and the nature of the claim.

Any documents in support of the application should be exhibited, including the medical reports.

10.3.4   Conditions to be satisfied

The court can make an order for an interim payment if:

(a)   the defendant against whom the order is sought has admitted liability to pay damages or some other sum of money to the claimant;

(b)   the claimant has obtained judgment against the defendant for damages to be assessed;

(c)   the court is satisfied that, if the claim went to trial, the claimant would obtain judgment for a substantial amount of money against the defendant from whom he or she is seeking an order for an interim payment and the defendant is insured in respect of the claim, or the defendant is a public body.

10.3.5   Compensation recovery

If the application is not a consent application and the defendant is liable to pay recoverable benefits, the defendant must obtain a certificate of recoverable benefits and a copy of the certificate should be filed at the hearing. The payment made to the claimant will be the net amount; however, for the purposes of the final judgment, the figure will be the gross amount.

10.3.6   Multi-defendants

Where there are multi-defendants, the court can make any order for interim payment of damages against any of them if:

(a)   it is satisfied that if the claim went to trial, the claimant would obtain judgment for substantial damages against at least one of the defendants;

(b)   each of the defendants is insured, covered by a MIB agreement or is a public body.

10.3.7   Amount of interim payment

CPR rule 25.7(4) states that the court must not order an interim payment of more than a reasonable proportion of the likely amount of final judgment. The court must take into account both contributory negligence and any relevant set-off or counterclaim. Where there is a possibility that the court will award periodical payments, the court must take care to ensure that the sum awarded does not impinge upon the court's ability to award periodical payments (*Cobham Hire Services v Eeles* [2009] EWCA Civ 204).

10.4   Key points

- Both a claimant and a defendant can make Part 36 offers to settle which have important consequences for costs.

- A properly constituted Part 36 offer remains open until it is withdrawn. A counter offer does not lead to a Part 36 offer lapsing.

- It is possible to bring other parties into an action by the use of Part 20 proceedings.

- A claimant can apply for an interim payment for part of the damages prior to trial.

10.5   Form

The following form is reproduced in full below:

10.5.1 Notice of offer to settle – Part 36 (N242A)

	Click here to reset form	Click here to print form

Notice of offer to settle - Part 36

Name of court *(If proceedings have started)*

Claim No.
(or other ref)

To the Offeree ('s Solicitor) *(Insert name and address)*

Claimant
(including ref)

Defendant
(including ref)

Take notice the (defendant)(claimant) offers to settle the claim. This offer is intended to have the consequences of Part 36. If the offer is accepted within _____ days (must be at least 21 days) of service of this notice the defendant will be liable for the claimant's costs in accordance with Rule 36.10 of the Civil Procedure Rules.

The offer is to settle:

(tick as appropriate)

☐ the whole of the claim

☐ part of the claim *(give details below)*

☐ a certain issue or issues in the claim *(give details below)*

The offer is:

(Insert details - expand box as necessary)

Note: Rule 36.5 specifies details that must be included in an offer including periodical payments of damages for future pecuniary loss.

Rule 36.11 requires that an offer by a defendant to pay a sum of money (other than periodical payments) must be paid within 14 days of acceptance.

☐ It (does)(does not) take into account all(part) of the following counterclaim:

(give details of the counterclaim)

Include only if claim for provisional damages

☐ The offer is made in satisfaction of the claim on the assumption that the claimant will not [develop (state the disease)] **OR** [suffer (state type of deterioration)].

But if that does occur, the claimant will be entitled to claim further damages at any time before (insert date).

OR

☐ This offer does not include an offer in respect of the claim for provisional damages.

To be completed by defendants only

☐ This offer is made without regard to any liability for recoverable benefits under the Social Security (Recovery of Benefits Act) 1997.

OR

☐ This offer is intended to include any relevant deductible benefits for which I am liable under the Social Security (Recovery of Benefits Act) 1997.

The amount of [£   ] is offered by way of gross compensation.

[I have not yet received a certificate of recoverable benefits]

OR

[The following amounts in respect of the following benefits are to be deducted (insert details).

Type of benefit   **Amount**

The net amount offered is therefore [£   ]]

Signed _____   Position held _____
Offeror('s solicitor)   (If signing on
                                        behalf of a firm
                                        or company)

Date _____

┌─────────────────────────────┐
│ **Click here to print form** │
└─────────────────────────────┘

11 Case Management, Disclosure and Inspection

This chapter looks at disclosure and inspection of documents under the CPR and issues relating to case management.

The period after the defence is filed is an important one. A party who understands principles of case management and can use these effectively can achieve a significant advantage over the less active party. At this stage, the parties have a duty to the court to assist in case management. However, to assist their clients, both sides should try to keep the momentum up, with the aim of securing a favourable settlement.

Case management is dealt with first. The directions made enable the court to identify and crystallise the issues and make any orders that may be needed. The important topic of disclosure of documents is then considered.

11.1 Case management

11.1.1 Case management tracks

The court is under a duty to manage cases. In the first instance, this involves allocating a case to a track:

(a) The small claims track normally involves cases with a value of less than £5,000. However, in personal injury cases the small claims track is only relevant where damages for PLSA are less than £1,000. There is a requirement therefore to state, in the claim form and in the particulars of claim, whether or not the claim for pain and suffering exceeds £1,000.

(b) The fast track involves cases where damages are less than £25,000 and the trial will take less than one day. If, for some reason, the trial will take more than one day, it is not suitable for allocation to the fast track.

(c)   The multi track involves cases of more than £25,000 or that are otherwise unsuitable for allocation to the fast track.

11.1.2   Allocation questionnaire

The first important document in a case is the allocation questionnaire (see Form N150 at para 11.8.1). This must be completed with care and returned within the period specified in the questionnaire.

11.1.3   Applications in course of proceedings

In straightforward cases, many practitioners will avoid making applications (eg for summary judgment, etc – see Chapter 13) and will seek to get the matter to trial. However, once it has been established that the application is, in fact, necessary, the solicitor should:

(a)   make the application in writing; alternatively, it may be prudent to wait and seek directions at the next case management conference;

(b)   consider whether the costs of the application can be justified (remember that an order for costs may be made against you);

(c)   ensure that the application has a realistic time estimate.

Making the application

The application is made on Form N244 (see para 11.8.2). The applicant must serve a copy of the notice on each respondent to the application together with any evidence relied upon, and a draft order should also be prepared and served. The applicant is required to state what the order is seeking and why the applicant is seeking the order. The evidence can be printed on the form and relied upon so long as it is supported by a statement of truth. The application must be served as soon as practicable after it is filed.

It is common for applications to be made by telephone. In these circumstances one party, usually the applicant, must arrange the telephone conference. That party must fix the conference for precisely the time fixed by the court, use one of a panel of approved telecommunication providers and gather all the contact details for the provider. The costs of arranging the call are part of the costs of the application (CPR Practice Direction 23A, para 6.10(8)).

Prior to the hearing, each party should serve a schedule of costs so that the court can assess costs at the end of the hearing.

When attending the application it is important that an order for costs is made. If there is no order for costs at all, then neither party can recover costs for attending.

Disclosure and inspection

Disclosure is the process by one party to the other of the existence of documents that are relevant to the issues in the case and which are not privileged. This process – which should in theory take place at the Pre-Action Protocol stage – is one that should enable the parties to test the strength of their cases and so perhaps encourage settlement.

Accordingly, this is an important topic, but is one that is often taken insufficiently seriously in personal injury claims because solicitors often feel it is unlikely that there will be any relevant documents.

Remember also that it is the solicitor's duty to obtain from the client and preserve any relevant documents, however embarrassing they may be to the client's case. The solicitor cannot be a party to such documents disappearing or not being disclosed (unless they are privileged). Disclosed documents may only be used for the purpose of the current proceedings, unless they have been read out in open court, or unless the party obtaining discovery applies to be released from the application.

Documents to look out for

(a)   The employer's accident book – look for entries regarding the current and previous similar accidents.

(b)   Risk assessment carried out by the employer or occupier.

(c)   The employer's complaints book.

(d)   Minutes of any safety committee.

(e)   Statements made to the employer or hospital after the accident if not made mainly with regard to future litigation.

(f)   Maintenance records of machine or vehicles involved in the accident.

(g)   The employee's sick notes.

(h)   The claimant's special damage documents, eg details of earnings, bonuses and sick pay.

11.1.4   Standard disclosure

CPR Part 31 deals with disclosure of documents and applies to both the fast and multi track. In most cases, all that is necessary is standard disclosure.

CPR rule 31.2 defines 'disclosure' as follows:

> A party discloses a document by stating that the document exists or has existed.

CPR rule 31.4 defines 'document' as follows:

> In this Part –
>
> 'document' means anything in which information of any description is recorded; and
>
> 'copy', in relation to a document, means anything onto which information recorded in the document has been copied, by whatever means and whether directly or indirectly.

CPR rule 31.5 makes it clear that, when a court makes an order to give disclosure, it is an order to give standard disclosure unless the court orders otherwise. Further, the court can dispense with or limit standard disclosure and the parties may agree in writing to dispense with or to limit standard disclosure.

CPR rule 31.6 defines 'standard disclosure' as follows:

> Standard disclosure requires a party to disclose only –
>
> (a) the documents on which he relies; and
>
> (b) the documents which –
>
>> (i)   adversely affect his own case;
>>
>> (ii) adversely affect another party's case; or
>>
>> (iii) support another party's case; and
>
> (c) the documents which he is required to disclose by a relevant practice direction.

11.1.5   Duty of search

The fact that standard disclosure takes place does not, however, mean that the litigator can afford to relax or that obligations to disclose can be ignored. CPR rule 31.7 imposes a duty on a party giving standard disclosure to make a reasonable search for documents falling within rule 31.6. The factors relevant in deciding the reasonableness of a search include:

(a)   the number of documents involved;

(b)   the nature and complexity of the proceedings;

(c)   the ease and expense of retrieval of any particular document; and

(d)   the significance of any documents which are likely to be located during the search.

Where a party has not searched for a category or class of document on the grounds that to do so would be unreasonable, he or she must state this in the disclosure statement and identify the category or class of document.

11.1.6   Duty of disclosure limited to documents which are or have been in party's control

A party's duty to disclose documents is limited to documents which are or have been in his or her control. This is defined as:

(a)   a document which is or was in the party's physical possession; or

(b)   a document which the party has or has had a right to possession of; or

(c)   a document which the party has or has had a right to inspect or take copies of.

11.1.7   Disclosure of copies

A party need not disclose more than one copy of a document. However, a copy of a document that contains a modification, obliteration or other marking feature, on which a party intends to rely or which adversely affects his or her case or another party's case or supports another party's case, is treated as a separate document.

11.2   Procedure for standard disclosure

Disclosure is by list, and CPR Practice Direction 31A, para 3.1 makes it clear that the list to be used is Form N265 (see para 11.8.3). The list must identify the documents in a convenient order and manner and as concisely as possible. It will normally be necessary to list the documents in date order, to number them consecutively and to give a concise description. Where a large number of documents fall into a particular category, they may be listed as a category rather than individually. The list must indicate those documents in respect of which the party claims a right or duty to withhold inspection, those documents which are no longer in the party's control, and must state what has happened to those documents.

11.2.1   Disclosure statement

The list must include a disclosure statement. This is a statement made by the party disclosing the documents:

(a)   setting out the extent of the search that has been made to locate documents of which disclosure is required;

(b)   certifying that he or she understands the duty to disclose documents;

(c)   certifying that to the best of his or her knowledge, he or she has carried out that duty.

Where the party making the disclosure statement is a company, firm, association or other organisation, the statement must also:

(a)   identify the person making the statement; and

(b)   explain why he or she is considered the appropriate person to make the statement.

11.2.2   Additional obligations

CPR Practice Direction 31A, para 4.2 states that the disclosure statement should:

(a)   expressly state that the disclosing party believes the extent of the search to have been reasonable in all the circumstances;

(b)   draw attention to any particular limitations on the extent of the search that were adopted for proportionality reasons and give the reasons why the limitations were not adopted, in setting out the extent of the search.

11.2.3   Agreement between parties

The parties may agree in writing to disclose documents without making a list and to disclose documents without the disclosing party making a disclosure statement.

11.2.4   Disclosure is a continuing obligation

Where the disclosing party is legally represented, that representative is under a duty to make sure that the person making the disclosing statement understands the duty of disclosure. The obligations continue until the proceedings end. If further documents come to the attention of the disclosing party, he or she must immediately notify every other party and prepare and serve a supplemental list.

11.3 Specific disclosure or inspection

CPR rule 31.12 allows the court to make an order for specific disclosure or specific inspection. CPR Practice Direction 31A, para 5.1 makes it clear that a party can apply for specific disclosure if he or she believes that disclosure given by the opposing party is inadequate. The application notice must specify the order that the applicant intends to ask the court to make and must be supported by evidence. The grounds on which the order is sought may be set out in the application itself but, if not, then it must be set out in the evidence in support.

The court will take into account all the circumstances of the case and, in particular, the overriding objective in **CPR Part 1**. The court may order the party to disclose documents specified in the order, and may order specific inspection of a document where the other party has stated in his or her disclosure statement that he or she will not permit inspection on the grounds that it would be disproportionate to do so.

11.4 Inspection and copying of documents

CPR rule 31.3 gives a party a right of inspection of a disclosed document except where:

(a) the document is no longer in the control of the party who disclosed it; or

(b) the party disclosing the document has a right or a duty to withhold inspection of it; or

(c) a party considers it would be disproportional to the issues in the case to permit inspection of documents within a category and states, in his or her disclosure statement, that inspection of those documents will not be permitted on the grounds that to do so would be disproportionate.

CPR rule 31.15 states that, where a party has a right to inspect a document, the party wishing to inspect must give written notice of his or her wish to inspect and the party who disclosed the document must permit inspection not more than 7 days after the date on which he or she received the notice.

CPR rule 31.15(c) states that a party seeking inspection may request a copy of the document, and if he or she also undertakes to pay reasonable copying costs, the party who disclosed the document must supply him or her with a copy not more than 7 days after the date on which he or she received the request.

11.5   Inadvertent disclosure of privileged documents

Privileged documents can only be disclosed with the permission of the court (CPR rule 31.20). Where privileged documents are disclosed inadvertently, a three-part test is applied:

(a)   whether it was evident to the solicitor receiving privileged documents that a mistake had been made. If it was, the solicitor should return the documents;

(b)   if it was not obvious, whether it would have been obvious to the reasonable solicitor that disclosure of these documents was a mistake. If it would, the privilege is retained. Where the case is close to the line, the solicitor should seek to ascertain whether an error has occurred;

(c)   if it would not have been obvious to the reasonable solicitor, privilege is lost.

11.5.1   Failure to disclose documents or permit inspection

CPR rule 31.21 states that a party may not rely on any document which he or she fails to disclose or in respect of which he fails to permit inspection unless the court gives permission.

11.5.2   Subsequent use of disclosed documents

CPR rule 31.22 reiterates the old law that a party to whom a document has been disclosed can only use it for the purpose of the proceedings in which it is disclosed, except where:

(a)   the document has been read to or by the court, or referred to, at a hearing which has been held in public;

(b)   the court gives permission;

(c)   the party who disclosed the document and the person to whom the document belongs agree.

The court has power to make an order restricting or prohibiting the use of a document which has been disclosed, even when it is read out in court or referred to at a hearing which has been held in public.

11.6 Disclosure in specific tracks

11.6.1 Fast track

Directions will be given on the allocation of a case to the fast track. These should include provision for the disclosure of documents and will *usually* be specified as standard disclosure. However, if the court does not consider this to be appropriate, it may direct that no disclosure take place or specify the documents to be disclosed. CPR Practice Direction 28, para 3.12 provides a typical timetable for fast track cases, giving 4 weeks after the notice of allocation for disclosure.

11.6.2 Multi track

The court must give directions and/or fix a case management conference when the case is allocated to the multi track. The directions must include an order as to disclosure. CPR Practice Direction 29, para 4.7 states that the court may limit the disclosure to standard or less and that the court may also direct that disclosure may take place by supplying copies of all documents, but the parties must either serve a disclosure statement with the copies or agree to disclose without such a statement.

11.7 Key points

- The court will manage the case in order to ensure that it proceeds expeditiously and fairly.

- A case will be allocated to a trial track. That track depends on the value of the case.

- The parties are under a duty to give disclosure of documents relevant to the case.

- Disclosure is a continuing obligation. There is a duty of search.

11.8   Forms

The following forms are reproduced in full below:

11.8.1 Allocation questionnaire (N150)

Click here to reset form | Click here to print form

Allocation questionnaire

To be completed by, or on behalf of,

Name of court

Claim No.

Last date for filing
with court office

who is [1st][2nd][3rd][   ][Claimant][Defendant]
[Part 20 claimant] in this claim

Please read the notes on page six before completing the questionnaire.

You should note the date by which it must be returned and the name of the court it should be returned to since this may be different from the court where the proceedings were issued.

If you have settled this claim (or if you settle it on a future date) and do not need to have it heard or tried, you must let the court know immediately.

Have you sent a copy of this completed form to the other party(ies)?   ☐ Yes   ☐ No

---

A Settlement

Under the Civil Procedure Rules parties should make every effort to settle their case before the hearing. This could be by discussion or negotiation (such as a roundtable meeting or settlement conference) or by a more formal process such as mediation. The court will want to know what steps have been taken. Settling the case early can save costs, including court hearing fees.

For legal representatives only

I confirm that I have explained to my client the need to try to settle; the options available; and the possibility of costs sanctions if they refuse to try to settle.   ☐

For all

Your answers to these questions may be considered by the court when it deals with the questions of costs: see Civil Procedure Rules Part 44.3 (4).

1. Given that the rules require you to try to settle the claim before the hearing, do you want to attempt to settle at this stage?   ☐ Yes   ☐ No

2. If Yes, do you want a one month stay?   ☐ Yes   ☐ No

3. Would you like the court to arrange a mediation appointment?   ☐ Yes   ☐ No

   (A fee will be payable to the mediation provider appointed by the National Mediation Helpline.)

4. If you answered 'No' to question 1, please state below the reasons why you consider it inappropriate to try to settle the claim at this stage.

Reasons:

N150 Allocation questionnaire (09.10)   1   © Crown copyright 2010

B Location of trial

Is there any reason why your claim needs to be heard at a particular court?   ☐ Yes   ☐ No

If Yes, say which court and why?

C Pre-action protocols

You are expected to comply with the relevant pre-action protocol.

Have you done so?   ☐ Yes   ☐ No

If No, explain why?

D Case management information

What amount of the claim is in dispute?   £

Applications

Have you made any application(s) in this claim?   ☐ Yes   ☐ No

If Yes, what for?
(e.g. summary judgment,
add another party)

For hearing on

Witnesses

So far as you know at this stage, what witnesses of fact do you intend to call at the trial or final hearing including, if appropriate, yourself?

Witness name	Witness to which facts

Experts

Do you wish to use expert evidence at the trial or final hearing?   ☐ Yes   ☐ No

Have you already copied any experts' report(s) to the other party(ies)?

☐ None yet obtained
☐ Yes   ☐ No

Do you consider the case suitable for a single joint expert in any field?   ☐ Yes   ☐ No

Please list any single joint experts you propose to use and any other experts you wish to rely on.
Identify single joint experts with the initials 'SJ' after their name(s).

Expert's name	Field of expertise (eg. orthopaedic surgeon, surveyor, engineer)

Do you want your expert(s) to give evidence orally at the trial or final hearing?   ☐ Yes   ☐ No

If Yes, give the reasons why you think oral evidence is necessary:

Track

Which track do you consider is most suitable for your claim? Tick one box

☐ small claims track
☐ fast track
☐ multi-track

If you have indicated a track which would not be the normal track for the claim,
please give brief reasons for your choice

3

Disclosure of electronic documents

If you are proposing that the claim be allocated to the multi-track:

1. Have you reached agreement, either using the Electronic Documents Questionnaire in PD31B or otherwise, about the scope and extent of disclosure of electronic documents on each side? ☐ Yes ☐ No

2. If No, is such an agreement likely? ☐ Yes ☐ No

3. If there is no agreement and no agreement is likely, what are the issues about disclosure of electronic documents which the court needs to address, and should they be dealt with at the Case Managment Conference or at a separate hearing?

E Trial or final hearing

How long do you estimate the trial or final hearing will take?

days	hours	minutes

Are there any days when you, an expert or an essential witness will not be able to attend court for the trial or final hearing? ☐ Yes ☐ No

If Yes, please give details

Name	Dates not available

F Proposed directions *(Parties should agree directions wherever possible)*

Have you attached a list of the directions you think appropriate for the management of the claim? ☐ Yes ☐ No

If Yes, have they been agreed with the other party(ies)? ☐ Yes ☐ No

G Costs

*Do **not** complete this section if you have suggested your case is suitable for the small claims track **or** you have suggested one of the other tracks and you do not have a solicitor acting for you.*

What is your estimate of your costs incurred to date? £

What do you estimate your overall costs are likely to be? £

In multi-track cases these questions should be answered in compliance with CPR Part 43.

H Fee

Have you attached the fee for filing this allocation questionnaire? ☐ Yes ☐ No

An allocation fee is payable if your claim or counterclaim exceeds £1,500.

Additional fees will be payable at further stages of the court process.

I Other information

Have you attached documents to this questionnaire? ☐ Yes ☐ No

Have you sent these documents to the other party(ies)? ☐ Yes ☐ No

If Yes, when did they receive them?

Do you intend to make any applications in the immediate future? ☐ Yes ☐ No

If Yes, what for?

In the space below, set out any other information you consider will help the judge to manage the claim.

Signed

[Counsel] [Solicitor] [for the][1st][2nd][3rd][   ]
[Claimant] [Defendant] [Part 20 claimant]

Date

Please enter your name, reference number and full postal address including (if appropriate) details of telephone, DX, fax or e-mail

	If applicable	
	Telephone no.	
	Fax no.	
	DX no.	
Postcode	Your ref.	

E-mail	

Click here to reset form | Click here to print form

Notes for completing an allocation questionnaire

- If the claim is not settled, a judge must allocate it to an appropriate case management track. To help the judge choose the most just and cost-effective track, you must now complete the attached questionnaire.
- If you fail to return the allocation questionnaire by the date given, the judge may make an order which leads to your claim or defence being struck out, or hold an allocation hearing. If there is an allocation hearing the judge may order any party who has not filed their questionnaire to pay, immediately, the costs of that hearing.
- Use a separate sheet if you need more space for your answers marking clearly which section the information refers to. You should write the claim number on it, and on any other documents you send with your allocation questionnaire. Please ensure they are firmly attached to it.
- The letters below refer to the sections of the questionnaire and tell you what information is needed.

A Settlement

Under the Civil Procedure Rules parties should make every effort to settle their case before the hearing. This could be by discussion or negotiation (such as a roundtable meeting or settlement conference) or by a more formal process such as mediation. The court will want to know what steps have been taken. If you think that it would be worthwhile you and the other party trying to negotiate a settlement at this stage you should tick the 'Yes' box. The court may order a stay, whether or not all the other parties to the claim agree. Even if you are requesting a stay, you should still complete the rest of the questionnaire.

More information about settlement options is available in the Legal Services Commission leaflet 'Alternatives to Court' free from any county court or the LSC leaflet line on 0845 3000 343. If you would like to find out more about mediation, and the fees charged, contact the National Mediation Helpline on 0845 60 30 809 or go to www.nationalmediationhelpline.com. Although you may appoint a mediator of your choice, if you would like the court to arrange a mediation for you please tick 'Yes'. By ticking this box you are consenting to your contact details being passed via the Helpline to an accredited external registered provider.

B Location of trial

High Court cases are usually heard at the Royal Courts of Justice or certain Civil Trial Centres. Fast or multi-track trials may be dealt with at a Civil Trial Centre or at the court where the claim is proceeding.

C Pre-action protocols

Before any claim is started, the court expects you to have complied with the relevant pre-action protocol, and to have exchanged information and documents relevant to the claim to assist in settling it. To find out which protocol is relevant to your claim see: http://www.justice.gov.uk/civil/procrules_fin/menus/protocol.htm

D Case management information

Applications

It is important for the court to know if you have already made any applications in the claim, what they are for and when they will be heard. The outcome of the applications may affect the case management directions the court gives.

Witnesses

Remember to include yourself as a witness of fact, if you will be giving evidence.

Experts

Oral or written expert evidence will only be allowed at the trial or final hearing with the court's permission. The judge will decide what permission it seems appropriate to give when the claim is allocated to track. Permission in small claims track cases will only be given exceptionally.

Track

The basic guide by which claims are normally allocated to a track is the amount in dispute, although other factors such as the complexity of the case will also be considered. Leaflet EX305 - The Fast Track and the Multi-track, explains this in greater detail.

E Trial or final hearing

You should enter only those dates when you, your expert(s) or essential witness(es) will not be able to attend court because of holiday or other commitments.

F Proposed directions

Attach the list of directions, if any, you believe will be appropriate to be given for the management of the claim. Agreed directions on fast and multi-track cases should be based on the forms of standard directions set out in the practice direction to CPR Part 28 and form PF52.

G Costs

Only complete this section if you are a solicitor and have suggested the claim is suitable for allocation to the fast or multi-track.

H Fee

For more information about court fees please go our website www.hmcourts-service.gov.uk or pick up a fees leaflet EX50 from any county court. If you cannot afford the fee, you may be eligible for remission of the fee. More details can be found in the leaflet EX160A, which can be downloaded from our website or you can pick up a copy from any county court.

I Other Information

Answer the questions in this section. Decide if there is any other information you consider will help the judge to manage the claim. Give details in the space provided referring to any documents you have attached to support what you are saying.

6

11.8.2 Application notice (N244)

Click here to reset form	Click here to print form

Application notice

For help in completing this form please read
the notes for guidance form N244Notes.

Name of court	
Claim no.	
Warrant no. (if applicable)	
Claimant's name (including ref.)	
Defendant's name (including ref.)	
Date	

1. What is your name or, if you are a solicitor, the name of your firm?

2. Are you a ☐ Claimant   ☐ Defendant   ☐ Solicitor
    ☐ Other *(please specify)*

    If you are a solicitor whom do you represent?

3. What order are you asking the court to make and why?

4. Have you attached a draft of the order you are applying for?   ☐ Yes   ☐ No

5. How do you want to have this application dealt with?   ☐ at a hearing   ☐ without a hearing
    ☐ at a telephone hearing

6. How long do you think the hearing will last?   [ ] Hours   [ ] Minutes

    Is this time estimate agreed by all parties?   ☐ Yes   ☐ No

7. Give details of any fixed trial date or period

8. What level of Judge does your hearing need?

9. Who should be served with this application?

N244 Application notice (05.08)   1   © Crown copyright 2008

10. What information will you be relying on, in support of your application?

☐ the attached witness statement

☐ the statement of case

☐ the evidence set out in the box below

If necessary, please continue on a separate sheet.

Statement of Truth

(I believe) (The applicant believes) that the facts stated in this section (and any continuation sheets) are true.

Signed _____   Dated _____

Applicant('s Solicitor)('s litigation friend)

Full name _____

Name of applicant's solicitor's firm _____

Position or office held _____
(if signing on behalf of firm or company)

11. Signature and address details

Signed _____   Dated _____

Applicant('s Solicitor)('s litigation friend)

Position or office held _____
(if signing on behalf of firm or company)

Applicant's address to which documents about this application should be sent

		If applicable
	Phone no.	
	Fax no.	
Postcode	DX no.	
	Ref no.	

E-mail address	

2

| Click here to print form |

Application Notice (Form N244) – Notes for Guidance

Court Staff cannot give legal advice. If you need information or advice on a legal problem you can contact Community Legal Service Direct on 0845 345 4 345 or www.clsdirect.org.uk, or a Citizens Advice Bureau. Details of your local offices and contact numbers are available via their website www.citizensadvice.org.uk

Paying the court fee

A court fee is payable depending on the type of application you are making. For example:

- To apply for judgment to be set aside
- To apply to vary a judgment or suspend enforcement
- To apply for a summons or order for a witness to attend
- To apply by consent, or without service of the application notice, for a judgment or order.

No fee is payable for an application by consent for an adjournment of a hearing if it is received by the court at least 14 days before the date of the hearing.

What if I cannot afford the fee?

If you show that a payment of a court fee would involve undue hardship to you, you may be eligible for a fee concession.

For further information, or to apply for a fee concession, ask court staff for a copy of the combined booklet and form EX160A - Court fees - Do I have to pay them? This is also available from any county court office, or a copy of the leaflet can be downloaded from our website www.hmcourts-service.gov.uk

Completing the form

Question 3

Set out what order you are applying for and why; e.g. to adjourn the hearing because..., to set aside a judgment against me because... etc.

Question 5

Most applications will require a hearing and you will be expected to attend. The court will allocate a hearing date and time for the application. Please indicate in a covering letter any dates that you are unavailable within the next six weeks.

The court will only deal with the application 'without a hearing' in the following circumstances.

- Where all the parties agree to the terms of the order being asked for;
- Where all the parties agree that the court should deal with the application without a hearing, or
- Where the court does not consider that a hearing would be appropriate.

Telephone hearings are only available in applications where at least one of the parties involved in the case is legally represented. Not all applications will be suitable for a telephone hearing and the court may refuse your request.

Question 6

If you do not know how long the hearing will take do not guess but leave these boxes blank.

Question 7

If your case has already been allocated a hearing date or trial period please insert details of those dates in the box.

Question 8

If your case is being heard in the High Court or a District Registry please indicate whether it is to be dealt with by a Master, District Judge or Judge.

Question 9

Please indicate in the box provided who you want the court to send a copy of the application to.

Question 10

In this section please set out the information you want the court to take account of in support of the application you are making.

If you wish to rely on:

- a witness statement, tick the first box and attach the statement to the application notice. A witness statement form is available on request from the court office.
- a statement of case, tick the second box if you intend to rely on your particulars of claim or defence in support of your application.
- written evidence on this form, tick the third box and enter details in the space provided. You must also complete the statement of truth. Proceedings for contempt of court may be brought against a person who signs a statement of truth without an honest belief in its truth.

Question 11

The application must be signed and include your current address and contact details. If you agree that the court and the other parties may communicate with you by Document Exchange, telephone, facsimile or email, complete the details

Before returning your form to the court

Have you:

- signed the form on page 2,
- enclosed the correct fee or an application for fee concession,
- made sufficient copies of your application and supporting documentation. You will need to submit one copy for each party to be served and one copy for the court.

11.8.3 List of documents: standard disclosure (N265)

List of documents: standard disclosure

Notes

- The rules relating to standard disclosure are contained in Part 31 of the Civil Procedure Rules.
- Documents to be included under standard disclosure are contained in Rule 31.6
- A document has or will have been in your control if you have or have had possession, or a right of possession, of it or a right to inspect or take copies of it.

In the	
Claim No.	
Claimant (including ref)	
Defendant (including ref)	
Date	

Click here to clear all fields

Click here to print form

Disclosure Statement

I, the above named

☐ Claimant   ☐ Defendant

☐ Party (if party making disclosure is a company, firm or other organisation identify here who the person making the disclosure statement is and why he is the appropriate person to make it)

state that I have carried out a reasonable and proportionate search to locate all the documents which I am

required to disclose under the order made by the court on (date of order)

☐ I did not search for documents:-

☐ pre-dating

☐ located elsewhere than

☐ in categories other than

☐ for electronic documents

☐ I carried out a search for electronic documents contained on or created by the following:
(list what was searched and extent of search)

N265 Standard disclosure (10.05)   HMCS

☐ I did not search for the following:-

☐ documents created before [   ]

documents contained on or created by the ☐ Claimant   ☐ Defendant

☐ PCs   ☐ portable data storage media
☐ databases   ☐ servers
☐ back-up tapes   ☐ off-site storage
☐ mobile phones   ☐ laptops
☐ notebooks   ☐ handheld devices
☐ PDA devices

documents contained on or created by the ☐ Claimant   ☐ Defendant

☐ mail files   ☐ document files
☐ calendar files   ☐ web-based applications
☐ spreadsheet files   ☐ graphic and presentation files

documents other than by reference to the following keyword(s)/concepts
(delete if your search was not confined to specific keywords or concepts)

[   ]

I certify that I understand the duty of disclosure and to the best of my knowledge I have carried out that duty. I further certify that the list of documents set out in or attached to this form, is a complete list of all documents which are or have been in my control and which I am obliged under the order to disclose.

I understand that I must inform the court and the other parties immediately if any further document required to be disclosed by Rule 31.6 comes into my control at any time before the conclusion of the case.

☐ I have not permitted inspection of documents within the category or class of documents (as set out below) required to be disclosed under Rule 31(6)(b)or (c) on the grounds that to do so would be disproportionate to the issues in the case.

[   ]

Signed [   ]   Date [   ]
(Claimant)(Defendant)('s litigation friend)

List and number here, in a convenient order, the documents (or bundles of documents if of the same nature, e.g. invoices) in your control, which you do not object to being inspected. Give a short description of each document or bundle so that it can be identified, and say if it is kept elsewhere i.e. with a bank or solicitor

I have control of the documents numbered and listed here. I do not object to you inspecting them/producing copies.

List and number here, as above, the documents in your control which you object to being inspected. (Rule 31.19)

I have control of the documents numbered and listed here, but I object to you inspecting them:

Say what your objections are

I object to you inspecting these documents because:

List and number here, the documents you once had in your control, but which you no longer have. For each document listed, say when it was last in your control and where it is now.

I have had the documents numbered and listed below, but they are no longer in my control.

11.8.4 Listing questionnaire (pre-trial checklist) (N170)

**Listing questionnaire
(Pre-trial checklist)** Click here to clear all fields

In the	

To be completed by, or on behalf of,

Claim No.	
Last date for filing with court office	

who is [1ˢᵗ][2ⁿᵈ][3ʳᵈ][ ][Claimant][Defendant]
[Part 20 claimant][Part 20 defendant] in this claim

Date(s) fixed for trial or trial period	

This form must be **completed** and **returned** to the court no later than the date given above. If not, your statement of case may be struck out or some other sanction imposed.

If the claim has settled, or settles before the trial date, you must let the court know immediately.

Legal representatives only: You must **attach** estimates of costs incurred to date, and of your likely overall costs. In substantial cases, these should be provided in compliance with CPR Part 43.

For multi-track claims only, you must also **attach** a proposed timetable for the trial itself.

A Confirmation of compliance with directions

1. I confirm that I have complied with those directions already given which require action by me. ☐Yes ☐No

   If you are unable to give confirmation, state which directions you have still to comply with and the date by which this will be done.

Directions	Date

2. I believe that additional directions are necessary before the trial takes place. ☐Yes ☐No

   If Yes, you should attach an application and a draft order.

   Include in your application all directions needed to enable the claim to be tried on the date, or within the trial period, already fixed. These should include any issues relating to experts and their evidence, and any orders needed in respect of directions still requiring action by any other party.

3. Have you agreed the additional directions you are seeking with the other party(ies)? ☐Yes ☐No

B Witnesses

1. How many witnesses (including yourself) will be giving evidence on your behalf at the trial? *(Do not include experts - see Section C)*

Continued over ➩

Witnesses continued

2. If the trial date is not yet fixed, are there any days within the trial period you or your witnesses would wish to avoid if possible? *(Do not include experts - see Section C)*

Please give details

Name of witness	Dates to be avoided, if possible	Reason

Please specify any special facilities or arrangements needed at court for the party or any witness (e.g. witness with a disability).

3. Will you be providing an interpreter for any of your witnesses? ☐ Yes ☐ No

C Experts

You are reminded that you may not use an expert's report or have your expert give oral evidence unless the court has given permission. If you do not have permission, you must make an application (see section A2 above)

1. Please give the information requested for your expert(s)

Name	Field of expertise	Joint expert?	Is report agreed?	Has permission been given for oral evidence?
		☐ Yes ☐ No	☐ Yes ☐ No	☐ Yes ☐ No
		☐ Yes ☐ No	☐ Yes ☐ No	☐ Yes ☐ No
		☐ Yes ☐ No	☐ Yes ☐ No	☐ Yes ☐ No

2. Has there been discussion between experts? ☐ Yes ☐ No

3. Have the experts signed a joint statement? ☐ Yes ☐ No

4. If your expert is giving oral evidence and the trial date is not yet fixed, is there any day within the trial period which the expert would wish to avoid, if possible? ☐ Yes ☐ No

If Yes, please give details

Name	Dates to be avoided, if possible	Reason

D Legal representation

1. Who will be presenting your case at the trial? ☐ You ☐ Solicitor ☐ Counsel

2. If the trial date is not yet fixed, is there any day within the trial period that the person presenting your case would wish to avoid, if possible? ☐ Yes ☐ No

If Yes, please give details

Name	Dates to be avoided, if possible	Reason

E The trial

1. Has the estimate of the time needed for trial changed? ☐ Yes ☐ No

If Yes, say how long you estimate the whole trial will take, including both parties' cross-examination and closing arguments ☐ days ☐ hours ☐ minutes

2. If different from original estimate have you agreed with the other party(ies) that this is now the **total** time needed? ☐ Yes ☐ No

3. Is the timetable for trial you have attached agreed with the other party(ies)? ☐ Yes ☐ No

Fast track cases only

The court will normally give you 3 weeks notice of the date fixed for a fast track trial unless, in exceptional circumstances, the court directs that shorter notice will be given.

Would you be prepared to accept shorter notice of the date fixed for trial? ☐ Yes ☐ No

F Document and fee checklist

Tick as appropriate

I attach to this questionnaire -

☐ An application and fee for additional directions ☐ A proposed timetable for trial

☐ A draft order ☐ An estimate of costs

☐ Listing fee

Signed	Please enter your [firm's] name, reference number and full postal address including (if appropriate) details of DX, fax or e-mail
[Counsel][Solicitor][for the][1st][2nd][3rd][ ] [Claimant][Defendant] [Part 20 claimant][Part 20 defendant]	
Date	
	Postcode

Tel. no.		DX no.		E-mail	
Fax no.		Ref. no.			

3 of 3

12 Preparing for Hearings: Disposals and Trial

This chapter considers the final steps needed to assemble the evidence and arrange for the case to be listed for trial and heard. As the trial itself is likely to be handled either by counsel or by a solicitor with some experience, it will not be dealt with here. The chapter also considers preparing for disposal hearings.

12.1 Disposal hearing

Where the claimant has a default judgment, the court will make directions to determine the amount to be paid. The court can make directions allocating the claim or order that the matter be heard by way of a 'disposal' hearing (CPR Practice Direction 26, para 12.4).

A disposal hearing will not normally last more than 30 minutes. The court will not normally hear oral evidence. It is prudent, therefore, for the parties to serve witness statements and to ensure that the schedules, counter schedules and medical evidence are up to date prior to the hearing. It is a requirement that the parties serve any written evidence at least 3 days prior to the hearing (CPR Practice Direction 26, para 12.4(5)).

Fast track trial costs do not apply to a case dealt with at a disposal hearing. The costs of a disposal hearing are at the discretion of the judge.

12.2 Preparing for trial

Any case not referred to a disposal should be regarded as a trial whether or not the claimant has judgment. The fact there is a judgment is not decisive of any issue in relation to any issue of damages (*Lunnun v Singh* [1999] CPLR 587). It is important, therefore, that the parties prepare thoroughly for any hearing, whether for damages to be assessed or whether there is an issue in relation to both liability and damages.

12.3 Instructing counsel to advise on evidence

It is often useful to have counsel's advice on evidence at an early stage in case additional evidence or directions are needed. However, in a case that will be argued by counsel, it is highly desirable for counsel to assess the available evidence at the latest once discovery is complete and well before the trial date. This is likely to be particularly important in more complex accidents-at-work cases where there is, for example, a conflict of engineering evidence.

Counsel will particularly need to see the proofs of evidence, documents disclosed on discovery, reports from experts, the police or the Health and Safety Executive, plans and photographs and an updated schedule of special damages. The advice should identify the witnesses to be called and the documents to be used, and should deal with any other outstanding matters such as hearsay notices, notices to admit, etc.

12.4 Documentary evidence

12.4.1 Documents

There may well be documents which the other party is unlikely to dispute if satisfied that they are genuine, for example, letters from the DSS and other special damage documentation. However, all documents not contained in witness statements, affidavits, expert opinion, given orally or as hearsay may be admitted provided notice is given. A counter notice, requiring the maker of the document to attend, may be served. Under CPR Part 31, a party is deemed to admit to the authenticity of a document disclosed unless he or she serves a notice that the document must be proved at trial (rule 32.19(1)).

12.4.2 Experts' reports

It is important that expert evidence is no more than one year old at most and, if necessary, obtain an updating report. The directions for using such evidence must have been obtained where necessary and complied with. An expert in the case cannot be used unless the court's permission has been given. It is advisable to try to agree the reports if possible. It may be helpful for experts to have a meeting before the trial in order to identify the areas in dispute. Often, the court will order this in any event. The experts will be expected to prepare a schedule setting out the issues on which they agree and disagree. On the fast track, the courts will be particularly keen to avoid experts giving evidence, so it is important to consider whether this is appropriate. There may be cases in which experts need to be called. See the section on expert evidence at para 9.5.

12.4.3 Plans and photographs

These should be exchanged and agreed if possible.

12.4.4 Previous convictions, etc

The defendant should be asked to admit the fact of the conviction if this has not already been done in the defence. If necessary, a notice to admit the fact can be served. As a precaution, the certificate of conviction should be obtained from the criminal court concerned. The defendant should be asked to agree that the coroner's notes of any inquest should be admissible.

12.4.5 Preparing bundles of documents

At least 14 days before the date set for trial, the defendant must notify the claimant of the documents he or she wants included in the trial bundle. The claimant must lodge the bundle no more than 7 or less than 3 days before the trial date. The bundles must be paginated and indexed.

The bundle must contain:

(a)   the claim form and all statements of case;

(b)   a case summary and/or chronology as appropriate;

(c)   requests for further information and the response to such requests;

(d)   all witness statements to be relied on as evidence;

(e)   any notices of intention to rely on hearsay evidence;

(f)   any medical report and responses to them;

(g)   any experts' reports and responses to them;

(h)   any order giving directions as to the conduct of the trial;

(i)   any other necessary documents.

The originals of the documents contained in the trial bundle together with copies of any other court orders should be available at court.

If the bundle is more than 100 pages, numbered dividers should be placed at intervals between groups of documents.

12.5   Witnesses

Drafting a witness statement is an important skill. In many cases, this will constitute the only evidence in chief which that witness is allowed to give. For this reason, more detailed guidance as to drafting witness statements can be found in Chapter 9.

12.5.1   Avoiding attendance of witnesses

Always try to avoid having to call witnesses by attempting to agree the evidence with the opponent. A means of putting pressure on the opponent to do so is to serve a notice to admit facts. The sanction is that, if the party served with the notice fails to admit the facts, he or she could be liable for the costs of proving those facts regardless of the outcome of the case. If a witness is too ill to travel or likely to die prior to the trial, there is a provision in CPR Part 34 for a witness to be examined prior to the trial by a judge or an examiner appointed by the court. Such deposition evidence is likely to be regarded as more powerful than evidence given by way of a witness statement. Where it is clear that such evidence would be beneficial, the solicitor should apply to the court specifying the details of the deponent. Where a witness has died or is going abroad for a long time, or cannot reasonably be expected to remember the events in question, then it should be possible, under section 1 of the Civil Evidence Act 1995, to rely on hearsay evidence. That is to say, where A told B about events that A had personally perceived, B's evidence may be admitted as 'first hand' hearsay.

If such hearsay evidence is to be used, then the procedure laid down in section 2 of the Civil Evidence Act 1995 must be followed, ie notice must be served of the intention to rely on such evidence to the court and the other parties to the action. This is implemented by CPR rule 33.2. If a party intends to rely on hearsay evidence contained in a witness statement, that statement must be served on the other parties. If no oral evidence is to be given in respect of the statement, the other parties must be informed of this with reasons for the non-attendance. This notice must be served no later than the last date of service of witness statements.

A counter notice of intent to challenge the hearsay evidence by attacking the credibility of the person who made the *original* statement, must be served within 14 days of service of the hearsay notice.

When seeking to admit or challenge hearsay evidence, section 4 of the Civil Evidence Act 1995 should be borne in mind. It deals with the weight the court should attach to hearsay evidence. Factors are: the reasonableness of the non-attendance at court of the maker of the original statement; whether the statement was contemporaneous; any motive of a person to conceal or misrepresent; and whether circumstances are such that a proper evaluation of the evidence is impossible due to non-attendance.

12.5.2 Witnesses who need to attend

In respect of those witnesses who will need to attend the trial, including the client, it is important to send them (in good time before the case may be heard) an updated proof of evidence for them to check and amend if necessary. As this will be the basis of the advocate's examination in chief of the witness, it should not contain any inadmissible material such as non-expert opinion or hearsay not covered by the Civil Evidence Act 1995. The witness should be asked to sign and date the proof in case he or she should die or become seriously ill before the trial, since the proof would then be admissible.

It should also be determined whether the witness is likely to attend the trial voluntarily.

If there is some doubt about this or, in some cases, if it will help the witness (such as some expert witnesses) to break other commitments, the witness should be served with a witness summons. To obtain a witness summons, under CPR Part 34, Form N20 should be completed. The witness may be served either personally or by post, a reasonable time before the trial.

12.5.3 Exchange of witness statements

The exchange of witness statements is mandatory (CPR rule 32.4). For the procedure for drafting a witness statement, see Chapter 9.

12.5.4 Expert witnesses

The fact that the court has given a party permission to rely upon a report from an expert does not mean that that party can call the expert to give evidence at trial. Under CPR rule 35.1(1) the parties must obtain permission to put in evidence an expert's report and call an expert. Care must be taken to ensure that the party has permission to call the expert if it is thought desirable to have that witness give evidence at trial: see para 9.5.

12.6   Real evidence

Arrangements must be made to bring to court vital objects that the judge may want to see in order to understand what is alleged to have occurred, for example, a defective brake part or the piece of machinery alleged to have caused the injury. If this is not feasible, for example, because of their size, and the position cannot be adequately explained by photographs, then it should be agreed with the other side that it will be necessary for the judge to view the object and/or accident scene in person, and to let the court know this in advance.

12.7   Other pre-trial points

12.7.1 Compliance with directions for trial

All pre-trial directions must be complied with.

12.7.2 Possible settlement of claim

It is still likely that the case will settle, even if only at the door of the court. However, beware the pressure that can be brought to bear on a claimant who has never been through court proceedings before. Most clients are apprehensive about giving evidence and worried about the court process.

12.7.3 Updating special damages calculation

Once updated figures are prepared, the claimant should try to agree them with the defence. Service of a notice to admit documents or a notice of intention of using hearsay evidence may encourage agreement.

12.7.4 Briefing counsel

Because of the need to be ready for trial as soon as the case is set down, it is advisable to prepare the brief at this stage. It is usual to instruct counsel who has been advising throughout, but the brief should be a full one so that the case can be taken over if necessary by new counsel.

The brief should enclose the statement of claim, reports, agreed bundles of documents, a schedule of special damages and previous opinions of counsel. It should outline the facts and the issues in dispute, the evidence and any difficulties with it, and any particularly salient or recent developments in the relevant law.

If no settlement is forthcoming, it will then be necessary to deliver the brief and to agree the brief fee. This is done over the telephone with counsel's clerk, professional ethics preventing counsel from dealing with the matter.

It may also be helpful for counsel to meet the client in conference at his or her chambers if this has not already occurred. This will convey to counsel the client's likely calibre as a witness, it should give the client added confidence in the person who will be his or her representative at the trial, and it may bring home to the client the difficulties in the case more effectively than advice from the solicitor with whom there is continuing contact.

12.7.5 Preparing schedule of costs

In a fast track trial, it is necessary for both parties to serve schedules of costs. This is also necessary in multi track cases where the hearing will be less than one day. The court will then assess costs at the end of the case. It is very important that these schedules are served and lodged at least 24 hours before the hearing.

12.8 Trial

12.8.1 Solicitor's role

This book assumes that the reader will not personally be presenting cases. The reader's role will, thus, be to ensure the attendance at court of the client and witnesses. In fast track cases, a solicitor will recover £345 for attending the trial if the court considers it necessary for the solicitor to be there to assist the advocate. If the solicitor does not attend, it is important to ensure that the advocate has all potential relevant documents. If the solicitor does attend the trial it will be necessary to liaise between the client and witnesses, on the one hand, and counsel on the other. It will also be necessary to take a note of the evidence, particularly when the advocate is on his or her feet.

12.8.2 After the judgment

It is important to remind the advocate to ask the judge to deal with the following matters where appropriate.

Interest on damages

Costs against the opponent – the judge should be asked to deal with any interlocutory applications where costs were reserved, and to point out where the client is entitled to costs whatever the outcome (for example, because of service of a notice to admit).

Part 36 offers

This may substantially affect the entitlement to costs. See Chapter 10.

Remaining matters

The following points may need attention:

(a)   If a party wishes to appeal, a notice of appeal must be served within 21 days (CPR rule 52.4).

(b)   Assessment of costs – if there is no assessment at the end of the trial, the judge will usually order that costs be assessed if not agreed. Try to agree costs, but, if this is not possible, remember that both parties can make offers in relation to costs.

12.9   Key points

- After judgment is entered, a court can order that a hearing is heard by way of a 'disposal'. Such a hearing will normally be no longer than half an hour and no evidence will be heard.

- Both parties must prepare carefully for trial. All evidence must be up to date and available at trial.

13 Early Conclusion of Cases

Most personal injury actions settle. This chapter deals with the most common means of settlement.

13.1 Settlement before or after proceedings issued

13.1.1 Settlement before proceedings have commenced

Many personal injury cases are settled without the need to start proceedings. The settlement terms are recorded in the correspondence between the solicitors and insurers. The latter may ask the claimant to sign a receipt confirming acceptance of the payment in full and final settlement of the claim. As problems of enforcement of settlements rarely arise in personal injury actions, no other formalities are needed except in the case of minors and other people under a disability, such as those with mental disability, where the court will have to approve the settlement.

However, it is important to explain the effect of a proposed settlement to the client. It is wise to obtain counsel's opinion on the proposed settlement in substantial cases. Written confirmation should be obtained from the client that he or she understands and accepts the settlement terms. Finally, it should be ensured that the position as to costs has been agreed.

13.1.2 Settlement after proceedings have commenced – informing the court

If the case has been allocated a trial date or trial window, the court must be informed of the settlement and the parties should jointly apply to withdraw the action.

Is a court order desirable?

An order has the advantages of certainty, and it will allow for costs to be taxed if they have not been agreed. The usual procedure is to obtain a stay of the proceedings, freezing them either temporarily or, once all the terms of the settlement have been agreed, permanently, except for the possibility of returning to court to ensure the carrying out of any of the terms agreed. This is referred to as a Tomlin order as it is named after the High Court Judge, Mr Justice Tomlin, following his ruling in *Dashwood v Dashwood* [1927] WN 276. The order should also refer to any interim payments already made, provide for payment out of any money in court, deal with which party is to receive the interest on money in court, and for costs between the parties and for assessment of any costs where the party is publicly funded.

Obtaining the consent order

The claimant will prepare a notice of application for judgment to be entered in the agreed terms, obtain the defendant's consent and then lodge it at court. The court will send sealed copies to both parties.

Money in court

The court will send the money in court to the claimant's solicitor on the making of the consent order.

13.2   Persons under a disability

When settling claims on behalf of minors and protected parties, the court's approval to the settlement will be needed before the settlement can be accepted if proceedings have started (CPR Part 21 Practice Direction, part 6). This is the same in fatal cases where a payment into court has to be apportioned between the Law Reform (Miscellaneous Provisions) Act 1934 and the Fatal Accidents Act 1976 claims and/or between dependants. An application is made by the Part 8 procedure if proceedings have not already begun. In all but the clearest cases, counsel's opinion on the merits of the settlement should be obtained. It is not wise to accept any suggestion by insurers that payment should be made simply against a receipt signed by the litigation friend; indeed, the insurers should be prepared to pay the claimant's costs in obtaining the court's approval.

13.2.1 Part 8 procedure

This is a special procedure for coming before the court when there is no substantial dispute as to facts or when an action is brought. It is used in cases such as:

(a)   minor approval summonses;

(b)   where a claim for provisional damages has been settled prior to issue but a court order is needed.

In these cases, the claimant must set out in the claim form:

(a)   details of what the court is being asked to decide;

(b)   details of any enactment relied upon;

(c)   whether the claimant or defendant is acting in a representative capacity.

In the High Court, applications for approval of settlement are made to masters and appointments are made in their own private rooms. The procedure is paralleled in county courts. If the claim is a simple one and the evidence is clear, counsel's opinion is not needed (CPR Practice Direction 21, para 5.2). Where there is any uncertainty over the settlement figure or the sum involved is large or needs apportioning under the Fatal Accidents Act 1976, then counsel's advice should be obtained. At the settlement hearing, the claimant's solicitor should have the application; a copy of CFO Form 320, completed on the first side, a copy of the child's birth certificate; any pleadings; if liability is disputed, evidence relating to liability; medical reports; schedule of damages and supporting documentation; consent of the litigation friend; and the approval of the settlement by the litigation friend. The litigation friend should attend. The test to be satisfied in order for the court to give its approval to the settlement is whether the settlement is a reasonable one and for the benefit of the infant or patient, having regard to all the circumstances of the case.

If the court does not approve the settlement, the application may be adjourned to give the parties further opportunities to negotiate. However, if it is approved, the order will direct by and to whom and in what amounts the money is to be paid and how the money is to be applied or otherwise dealt with. The next friend can, however, apply for payment of expenses and for payments for the child's benefit, such as alterations to the home or a holiday to help recuperation. The claimant's money will be invested until he or she is old enough to manage his or her own affairs save for the necessary expenditure to maintain the claimant whilst he or she is under a disability. If the claimant is a protected party the settlement moneys will usually be transferred to the Court of Protection.

In cases where the settlement is approved, the usual order is to direct costs to be assessed on the standard basis.

13.3   Default judgments: summary judgment

13.3.1 Default judgments

Judgment can be obtained if the defendant fails to file an acknowledgment of service or defence within the proper time. Such judgment will be judgment on liability with damages and interest to be assessed later and costs to be assessed.

Note that the leave of the court will be needed if the defendant is under a disability or the claimant is claiming provisional damages.

Such default judgments may be set aside on the application of the defendant, but the defendant will usually have to show a good reason for allowing the judgment to be entered (such as illness) and that there is a possible defence.

13.3.2 Summary judgment (CPR Part 24)

Either the claimant or defendant may apply for summary judgment. The grounds for summary judgment are that the claimant/defendant has no reasonable grounds of succeeding or successfully defending the claim or issue, and there is no other reason why the case should not be disposed of at trial (*Swain v Hillman & Gay* [2000] PIQR P51).

The application can be made at the time of issue after the filing of either the acknowledgement of service or a defence. If an application for summary judgment is made after filing of the acknowledgement of service, it will stay the filing of the defence. Summary judgment is ideally sought when the claimant files his allocation questionnaire after service of defence and before the claim is allocated to the relevant track. The application is made on notice; this must include a statement that it is an application for summary judgment and made under CPR Part 24. The notice must identify concisely any point of law or provision in the document on which the application relies and it must state that the application is made because the applicant believes that on the evidence the respondent has no real prospect of success. The applicant must state that he or she knows of no reason why the matter should not proceed to trial. Thus, when making the application, the solicitor must be quite clear that he or she has researched all the avenues of evidence. The respondent must be given 14 days' notice of the date fixed for the hearing and the issues it is proposed that the court will deal with on the application. Furthermore, the respondent must file evidence in reply at least 7 days before the hearing. Evidence in reply from the applicant must be filed at least 3 working days prior to the hearing.

The court may make conditional orders; however, it is unclear what powers the court has in relation to the defendant. If the claimant is successful in obtaining summary judgments on liability, provision will need to be made to assess damages. The matter will go to a case management hearing for directions for this purpose.

13.3.3 Judgment on admissions

If the defendant admits both liability and the fact that the claimant has suffered some damage, whether in the pleadings, correspondence or otherwise, the claimant can proceed to obtain judgment (CPR rule 14.6(4)). The request found at the foot of Form N205(b) may be adapted for this purpose if the court does not supply an appropriate 'practice form'. If the defendant admits liability, he or she may do so by filing a notice on Form N9C which provides for admission of liability with application for the court to determine the amount or with an offer to pay a specified sum. This form is designed for the individual defendant and is not appropriate for an insurance company. This will normally be judgment on liability only as above.

13.4　Striking out, dismissal for want of prosecution, discontinuance

13.4.1 Striking out by the court

The court has the power to strike out all or part of a statement of case under CPR rule 3.4(1). This can be done if it discloses no reasonable grounds for bringing or defending the claim, that it is an abuse of the court's process or is otherwise likely to obstruct the just disposal of the proceedings, or that there has been a failure to comply with a rule, practice direction or court order.

The court may strike out of its own motion, or upon application by any party. If the court has struck the matter out of its own initiative, the order must state that the affected party may apply to have it set aside, varied or stayed. If the court does not specify a time limit in which to apply to set aside, it must be done within 7 days after service of the order.

13.4.2 Dismissal for want of prosecution

The courts have power to do this inherently and under several rules. This is a key defence tactic to deal with cases which the claimant accidentally or deliberately has let 'go to sleep', although it is not used as much as formerly. Prior to the CPR, the defendant could apply for the action to be dismissed for want of prosecution if it could be shown that the claimant's delay was either intentional and contumelious (insolent) (for example, deliberate disobedience to a peremptory order of the court); or that it is inordinate, inexcusable and prejudicial to the fair trial of the action. The whole period of the delay must be looked at and the nearer the limitation period is to expiry the quicker the claimant must act. However, if the limitation period has not expired, the action will not *usually* be dismissed since the claimant could start another action (*Birkett v Janes* [1978] AC 297).

These principles established under the old law are unlikely to have much relevance to the CPR, with the sanctions they provide at every stage, although there may remain cases of delay where the principles above have relevance. Under the CPR, the court now has wide powers to deal with non-compliance with time limits and it can make orders which, in many cases, will be more appropriate in dealing with the claimant's delay than the draconian measure of striking out (*Biguzzi v Rank Leisure plc* [1999] 1 WLR 1926). The alternatives include orders for costs and orders depriving the claimant of part of the interest on any damages.

13.4.3 Discontinuance (CPR Part 38)

The claimant may discontinue an action at any time; however, costs are usually awarded against the discontinuing party. Where a claimant has received an interim payment, he or she can only discontinue if the defendant who made the payment consents in writing or the court gives its permission. To discontinue, the claimant must file with the court and serve notice of the discontinuance on every party. The defendant has the right to have the notice set aside in certain circumstances, but this application must be made within 28 days of service of the notice of discontinuance. Discontinuance takes effect on the date when the notice is served and the defendant will be entitled to his or her costs to the date of service of notice.

13.5   Key points

- Most cases settle without the need to issue proceedings.

- A court order approving a settlement is only needed if the claimant is a person under a disability.

- A claimant can obtain judgment without a trial by entering judgment in default, or by applying for summary judgment or for judgment on admissions.

14 Summary of Procedure

14.1 Determining value of claim

(a) No account is taken of any possible finding of contributory negligence – unless that negligence is admitted.

(b) No account is taken of interest.

(c) If the claimant is seeking an award for provisional damages, no account will be taken of the possibility of a future application for such damages.

(d) Costs are not taken into account.

(e) Moneys liable to recoupment by the DSS' CRU are taken into account.

14.2 Small claims track

The small claims track limit is now governed by the issue of whether or not general damages for pain and suffering exceeds £1,000. It is necessary to state that the claim for pain and suffering exceeds this figure.

14.2.1 Where claim can be issued

A personal injury action can be launched in any county court. When the defendant files an acknowledgement of service, he or she can apply to have the action transferred to his or her home court. Furthermore, either party may apply to the court for the transfer of proceedings to another court under CPR rule 30.2 or may specify their preferred court in the allocation questionnaire.

14.2.2 Drafting particulars of claim

The claim form must clearly state the value of the claim. The purpose of this is to enable the court to allocate the claim to the relevant track. The small claims track is for claims for personal injury valued at less than £1,000, total damages sought not to exceed £5,000. The fast track is the usual track for claims where damages for the personal injury have a value of more than £5,000 but the total value of the claim is less than £25,000. The multi track is for claims over £25,000.

14.2.3 Service

If the court does not serve proceedings, the claimant's solicitor must serve the claim form and particulars of claim within 4 months after the date of issue of the claim form. The claim form may be served by post; particular care must be taken to ensure that service takes place at the nominated address for service or on the nominated solicitor.

14.2.4 Documents to be served with particulars of claim

The following documents must accompany the particulars of claim:

(a)   a medical report;

(b)   a statement of the special damages claimed.

14.3   Case management directions

When the defendant files a defence, the court will serve an allocation questionnaire on each party. Once the allocation questionnaires have been filed, or the time for filing has expired, the court will allocate a claim to a track and will serve notice of allocation on every party.

14.3.1 Fast track directions

On allocation to the fast track, the court will fix a trial date and tailor its directions to individual cases. A timetable will be set for those steps to be taken. Directions will include:

(a)   disclosure (usually standard, although the court may direct that no disclosure is to take place or specify the class of documents to be disclosed);

(b)   service of witness statements; and

(c)   expert evidence.

A typical timetable from the date of notice of allocation the court may give for preparation of the case is as follows:

Disclosure	4 weeks
Exchange of witness statements	10 weeks
Exchange of experts' reports	14 weeks
Sending of listing questionnaires by the court	20 weeks
Filing of completed listing questionnaires	22 weeks
Hearing	30 weeks

14.3.2 Multi track directions

On allocation to the multi track, the court will issue case management directions and a timetable for those steps to be taken. The court will also fix a case management conference or a pre-trial review or both, as well as fixing a trial date or period in which the trial is to take place. The essence of the multi track is flexibility and, as such, there are no specimen or standard directions. This track deals with claims of higher value, claims which cannot be dealt with in one day and complex claims. Where the claim is not complex, the court will give similar directions to those applied in fast track claims.

Directions the court must give on listing are as follows:

(a)   The court must fix a trial date or week, give a time estimate and fix the place.

(b)   The parties should seek to agree directions and may file an agreed order. The court may make an order in those terms or it may make a different order.

(c)   Agreed directions should include provision about:

   (i)   evidence, especially expert evidence;

   (ii)   a trial timetable and a time estimate;

   (iii) the preparation of a trial bundle;

   (iv)   any other matter needed to prepare the case for trial.

14.3.3 Preparing bundle for trial

The parties should receive at least 21 days' notice of the hearing. Where possible, the parties should agree the contents of the bundle. Not more than 7 days and not less than 3 days before the start of the trial, the claimant must file the trial bundle, which must be paginated, indexed and contained in a ring binder. The bundle should include the claim form and all statements of case, witness statements, requests for further and better particulars and experts' reports. Identical bundles should be supplied to all the parties to the proceedings and for the use of witnesses.

15 Avoiding the Pitfalls of Personal Injury Litigation

Personal injury litigation has many areas where problems can occur for the litigator. This chapter looks at the key problems and how to avoid them.

15.1 Funding

It is important that the funding of litigation is considered in detail at the outset.

15.1.1 Pre-existing legal insurance

Rigorous steps must be taken to discover whether the claimant has pre-existing legal insurance or other means of funding the litigation, such as trade union assistance.

15.1.2 Conditional fee agreement

A claimant lawyer must ensure that the claimant understands the conditional fee agreement, the costs and the nature of the insurance taken out.

15.1.3 Notifying the defendant

It is essential that the defendant and the relevant insurer are informed at the outset that the matter is being conducted under a conditional fee agreement and that an insurance policy has been taken out.

15.2 Limitation

Limitation is a major area of problems for claimants.

15.2.1 Failure to note that limitation period is imminent

The issue of when the limitation period expires is one of the first issues that a claimant lawyer must consider when instructed. This must be noted and a central log of limitation periods kept.

15.2.2 Claimant gives wrong limitation period

It is not unusual for claimants to give the wrong date for an accident when giving initial details to their solicitor. The claimant's account must be checked against contemporary records, particularly medical records.

15.2.3 Arguments over date of knowledge

Problems with the date of knowledge of the claimant often occur in industrial disease and clinical negligence cases. It is wise for a claimant lawyer to be aware of potential problems from the outset. In particular, medical notes and records should be checked as soon as possible.

15.2.4 Limitation periods other than 3 years

Claimants are often caught out by the fact that some limitation periods are not 3 years and some can have shorter periods, such as:

- accidents abroad;
- accidents in the air (or at airports);
- accidents at sea.

See para 2.5.4. This fact must be noted and identified by the claimant lawyer at once.

15.2.5 If limitation period is missed

In some (but not all) cases the court may have a discretion under section 33 of the Limitation Act 1980 to allow the matter to proceed. In such cases, proceedings should be issued at once and an application made promptly.

15.3   Pre-Action Protocol

It is important that the claimant and defendant both comply with the letter and spirit of the Pre-Action Protocol.

15.3.1 Proper notification by claimant

A full and appropriate letter of claim must be sent (see paras 7.3.2 and 7.10).

15.3.2 Proper response by defendant

The defendant should, within 3 months, state whether or not liability is admitted. If liability is denied, or contributory negligence alleged, then disclosure should be made (see para 7.3.3).

15.3.3 Failure to comply with Pre-Action Protocol

A failure by the claimant or defendant to comply with the Pre-Action Protocol can lead to cost penalties. A claimant faced with a defaulting defendant can issue an application for pre-action disclosure.

15.3.4 Insufficient time to comply with Pre-Action Protocol

The fact that the parties are conducting the case under the Pre-Action Protocol does not extend the limitation period. If there is insufficient time to comply with the Protocol, then the claimant should issue and apply to the court for directions in order that the parties have the opportunity to go through the stages of the Protocol.

15.4 Problems on issue

Many problems can occur upon issue.

15.4.1 Claimant must ensure that proper defendant is served

If there is any doubt as to whether the proper defendant has been served, the claimant should use the Pre-Action Protocol period to invite the defendant to clarify this issue. If the wrong defendant is sued, an application can be made to name the correct defendant.

15.4.2 Claimant must ensure that defendant is appropriate legal defendant

Problems can occur if the defendant is a company that is insolvent, a bankrupt or a club. A company search should be made before issue.

15.5   Problems with service

Once proceedings are issued, the question of service is another area fraught with potential problems for the claimant.

15.5.1   Claim form not served within 4 months of date of issue

A failure to serve means that the action cannot proceed. It is dangerous to apply for an extension of time because this may not be granted and the defendant can apply to set such an order aside. If there is a problem with service (for instance, because the medical report or particulars are not available), the claim form should be served and an extension of time for service of the other documents should be applied for.

15.5.2   Claim not served appropriately

A common error is to fail to notice that a solicitor has stated that he or she will accept service. It must be ensured that the correct method of service is marked on the file or otherwise noted.

15.5.3   Incorrect method of service adopted

The claimant may be able to serve the claim form again if the matter is still within the initial 4-month period, in which case a sealed copy of the claim form must be served. If the matter is outside the 4-month period and the defendant notices this and makes an appropriate application to set aside service, there is little that the claimant can do in response.

15.5.4   Potential pitfall for defendant

A defendant who wishes to take issue as to whether appropriate service has taken place must return the acknowledgment of service stating that jurisdiction is to be disputed and then issue an application to dispute the jurisdiction. Any other step, for instance filing a defence stating that service is to be disputed, in itself represents acceptance of the jurisdiction and the defendant cannot then dispute issues relating to service.

15.6   Problems with defendant insurers or the Motor Insurers' Bureau

In a road traffic accident case, it is important that the defendant insurer is given appropriate notification under the RTA 1988.

15.6.1 Notice to the insurer under RTA 1988, section 151

The claimant must give the insurer notice of issue to the insurer under section 151 of the RTA 1988 before the issue of proceedings or within 7 days of notice.

15.6.2 Notice not given

If notice is not given and the defendant's insurer indicates that it will not provide an indemnity, it is possible to discontinue the first action and issue again (giving appropriate notice on this occasion).

15.6.3 Potential problems with Motor Insurers' Bureau

The MIB requirements are dealt with at para 15.10. If the claimant has failed to give appropriate notice to the MIB prior to service and the MIB indicates that this is an issue, the only effective remedy is to discontinue the action and issue again, giving appropriate notice on this occasion. This is possible even if the limitation period has expired. The court still has a discretion under section 33 of the Limitation Act 1980 (see *Richardson v Watson* [2006] EWCA Civ 1662).

15.7 Problems after service

The claimant must make sure that the dates for filing the acknowledgment of service and defence are noted and judgment is entered if they are not filed.

15.7.1 Complying with all directions of the court

Both parties must diarise the date of court orders and compliance.

15.7.2 Problems with timetable

Whilst the parties can agree to extend some parts of the timetable it is prudent to confirm this in writing. It is unlikely that a court will change the trial date once it is set. Any agreement to extend time must make sure that the parties are still ready for trial.

15.7.3 Failure to file allocation questionnaire or listing questionnaire

The court may strike out the claim or defence if the parties do not file the allocation questionnaire or listing questionnaire. Particular care must be taken to ensure that these documents are filed on time and completed appropriately.

15.8   Avoiding problems for client

It is important that the client is kept informed of the progress of the case.

15.8.1 Complete and accurate client's statement

The statement must be in the client's own words and deal with both liability and damages.

15.8.2 Making client aware of importance of statement of truth

A false statement could lead to an application for contempt of court proceedings; as such, it is important that the claim is not exaggerated and is accurate.

15.9   Part 36 offers

Both parties can make Part 36 offers to settle the case.

15.9.1 Making client aware of consequence of Part 36 offer

A claimant, in particular, must be made aware of the consequences in relation to costs (see para 10.1.6).

15.9.2 Withdrawing offer if circumstances change

An offer remains open until it is withdrawn, even if a counter offer is made. If it becomes clear to a claimant who has made an offer that the action has a higher value than the offer that has been made then the offer should be expressly withdrawn. Similarly, a defendant must expressly withdraw an offer to the claimant if it appears that the claim has a lower value. Until such time as the offer is withdrawn it can be accepted. (This does not apply if the offer is time limited.)

15.10 Motor Insurers' Bureau

The MIB uninsured driver's agreement (the Agreement) came into force on 1 October 1999. This places onerous duties on claimant lawyers, particularly in cases where the MIB is not joined in the action at the outset.

15.10.1 Cases in which Motor Insurers' Bureau is not a party at the outset

Conditions precedent to Motor Insurers' Bureau's liability

The Agreement states that the MIB shall incur no liability unless application is made to the person specified in clause 9(1):

(a)   in such form;

(b)   giving such information about the relevant proceedings and other matters relevant to the agreement; and

(c)   accompanied by such documents as the MIB may reasonably require.

Service of notices on Motor Insurers' Bureau

Notice will *only* be sufficiently given if by fax or by registered or recorded delivery to the MIB's registered office. Delivery shall be proved by the production of a fax transmission report produced by the sender's facsimile machine or an appropriate postal receipt.

Clause 9 of the Agreement: the need to give proper notice

Clause 9(1) of the Agreement states that the MIB shall not incur liability unless proper notice is given within 14 days of the commencement of proceedings (in cases where an insurer with a relevant interest can be identified) to that insurer, or in any other case to the MIB.

'Proper notice'

Careful note must be taken of the matters that must be produced to show 'proper notice':

(a)   Notice in writing that proceedings have been issued by claim form, writ or other means:

   (i)   a copy of the sealed claim form, writ or other official documents;

(ii)   evidence of the commencement of the proceedings.

(b)   A copy or details of any insurance policy providing benefits in the case of the death, bodily injury or damage to property to which the proceedings relate where the claimant is the insured party and the benefits are available to him or her.

(c)   Copies of all correspondence in the possession of the claimant or his solicitor or agent to or from the defendant, his solicitor or agents which is relevant to:

    (i)   the death, bodily injury or damage for which the defendant is alleged to be responsible;

    (ii)   any contract of insurance which covers, or which may or which has been alleged to cover, liability for such death, injury or damage the benefit of which is, or is claimed to be, available to the defendant.

(d)   A copy of the particulars of claim, whether served or not.

(e)   A copy of all other documents which are required under the appropriate rules of procedure to be served on the defendant with the claim form, writ or other originating process or with the particulars of claim.

(f)   Such other information about the relevant proceedings as the MIB may reasonably specify.

Clause 9(3) of the Agreement states:

> If in the case of proceedings commenced in England or Wales, the Particulars of Claim (including any document required to be served therewith) has not yet been served with the Claim Form or other originating process paragraph (2)(e) shall be sufficiently complied with if a copy thereof *is* served on N1113 not later than seven days after it is served on the Defendant.

Notice of service of proceedings

Note that there are two obligations:

(a)   to give notice of issue;

(b)   to give notice of service.

Clause 10(2) of the Agreement states that the MIB will not incur liability unless notice, in writing, is given within 7 days of service, ie 7 days after:

(a)   the date when the defendant received notification from the court that service has occurred;

(b)   the date when the claimant received notification from the defendant that service of the claim form or other originating process has occurred;

(c)   the date of personal service.

Or the appropriate date can mean:

(d)   14 days after the date when service is deemed to have occurred in accordance with the CPR,

whichever of these dates occurs first.

Yet more information

The MIB is not liable unless the claimant, within 7 days of any of the following events, gives notice to the MIB or insurer concerned:

(a)   the filing of a defence;

(b)   any amendment of the particulars of claim or any amendment of or addition to any schedule or other document required to be served therewith; and

(c)   either the setting down of the action or, where the court gives notice to the claimant of the trial date, the date when that notice is received.

The MIB must also be sent copies of the documents within 7 days.

Note: the requirement to file documents could be construed to include supplementary letters from doctors.

'Catch-all'

Clause 11(2) of the Agreement states that the MIB shall not incur any liability unless the claimant (which includes his or her solicitors) furnishes such further information and documents in support of the claim as the MIB may reasonably require, notwithstanding that the claimant may have complied with all the earlier obligations.

Applying for judgment

Clause 12 of the Agreement states that the MIB shall incur no liability unless the claimant, after commencement of the proceedings, and not less than 35 days before the appropriate date, has given notice in writing of his intention to apply for judgment.

Clause 13 of the Agreement

Clause 13 states that the MIB shall not be liable unless the claimant *has as soon as reasonably practicable* demanded the information specified in section 154(1) of the RTA 1988 (ie a request to give particulars of insurance). If the person of whom demand is made fails to comply with the provisions of section 154, a formal complaint must be made to a police officer and the name and address of the registered keeper of the vehicle should be obtained.

Duty to pursue other parties

Clause 14(1) of the Agreement states that the MIB shall incur no liability under MIB's obligation unless the claimant has, if so required by the MIB (and upon the MIB giving an indemnity as to costs), taken all reasonable steps to obtain judgment against every person who may be liable (including any person who may be vicariously liable) in respect of the claim.

Do not refuse to consent

Similarly, clause 14(2) of the Agreement states that the MIB shall incur no liability if the claimant, upon being requested to do so by the MIB, refuses to consent to the MIB being joined as a defendant to the relevant proceedings.

Assignment of judgment and undertakings

Clause 15 of the Agreement states that the MIB shall incur no liability unless the claimant has assigned to the MIB or its nominee the unsatisfied judgment and undertaken to repay to the MIB any sums paid to him or her subsequently received.

Compensation received from other sources

Clause 17 of the Agreement states that where a claimant has received compensation from the Policyholders Protection Board or an insurer under an agreement or arrangement or any other source in respect of the death, bodily injury or other damage to which the relevant proceedings relate and such compensation has not been taken into account in the calculation of the relevant sum, the MIB may deduct from the relevant sum an amount equal to that compensation.

15.10.2 Cases in which Motor Insurers' Bureau is a party to the proceedings

Some of these requirements are relaxed if the MIB is a party to the action at the outset. In these circumstances, the particulars of claim *must* contain the wording required by the MIB as to the MIB's position. Only some of the requirements are relaxed.

It is still necessary:

(a) to give notice of relevant proceedings not later than 14 days after issuing proceedings;

(b) to give notice of service on the defendant within 7 days;

(c) to serve a copy of the defence within 14 days of the claimant receiving it;

(d) to give full notice of intention to apply for judgment.

Whether or not the MIB is a party, actions involving the MIB must be conducted with extreme care.

Appendix 1
Useful Addresses

Action against Medical Accidents

44 High Street
Croydon
Surrey CR0 1YB
tel: 0845 123 23 52
www.avma.org.uk

Association of Consulting Engineers

Alliance House
12 Caxton Street
London SW1H OQL
tel: 0207 222 6557
email: consult@acenet.co.uk
www.acenet.co.uk

Association of Personal Injury Lawyers

3 Alder Court
Rennie Hogg Road
Nottingham NG2 1RX
tel: 0115 958 0585
www.apil.org.uk

Compensation Recovery Unit

Durham House
Washington
Tyne and Wear NE38 7SF
email: cru-info-management@dwp.gsi.gov.uk

Criminal Injuries Compensation Authority

Tay House
300 Bath Street
Glasgow G2 4LN
tel: 0800 358 3601
www.cica.gov.uk

HSE Information

Caerphilly Business Park
Caerphilly CF83 3GG
tel: 0845 345 0055
email: hse.infoline@connaught.plc.uk
www.hse.gov.uk

Medical Defence Union

MDU Services Limited
230 Blackfriars Road
London SE1 8PJ
tel: 08444 20 20 20
email: mdu@the-mdu.com
www.the-mdu.com

Medical Protection Society

33 Cavendish Square
London W1G OPS
tel: 0845 605 4000
email: info@mps.org.uk
www.medicalprotection.org

Motor Insurers' Bureau

Linford Wood House
6–12 Capital Drive
Linford Wood
Milton Keynes MK14 6XT
tel: 01908 830001
email: Enquiries@mib.org.uk
www.mib.org.uk

Appendix 2
Further Reading

Allen, S, Bowley I and Davies, H, *The APIL Guide to Damages* (Jordan Publishing Limited, 2nd edn, 2008).

Cotter, B and Bennett, D, *Munkman on Employer's Liability* (Butterworths, 15th edn, 2009).

Curran, P, Williams, V and Gore, A, *Personal Injury Pleadings* (Sweet & Maxwell, 4th edn, 2008).

Exall, G, *Munkman on Damages for Personal Injuries and Death* (Butterworths, 11th edn, 2004).

Exall, G, *The APIL Guide to Fatal Accident Claims* (Jordan Publishing Limited, 2009).

Ford, N and Clarke, J, *Redgrave's Health and Safety* (Butterworths, 7th edn, 2010).

Foster, C and Bradley, B, *The APIL Guide to Tripping and Slipping Cases* (Jordan Publishing Limited, 2010).

McGee, A, *Limitation Periods* (Sweet & Maxwell, 6th edn, 2010).

Padley, C and Begley, L, *Criminal Injuries Compensation Claims* (Law Society, 2005).

Pether, M, Cargill, V, Graham, R et al, *Bingham and Berryman's Personal Injury and Motor Claims Cases* (Butterworths, 13th edn, 2010).

Evidence

Hollander, C, *Documentary Evidence* (Sweet & Maxwell, 10th edn, 2009).

Iller, M, *Civil Evidence: The Essential Guide* (Sweet & Maxwell, 2006).